Exploring Physical Science

Exploring

ENERGY

Andrew Solway

rosen publishing's
rosen central®

New York

Published in 2008 by The Rosen Publishing Group, Inc.
29 East 21st Street, New York, NY 10010

First Edition

Cover photograph: NASA

Photo credits: p. 5: Chris Fairclough/cfwimages.com; p. 6: Discovery Books; p. 8: NASA/JPL-
Caltech/S. Wilner; p. 9: Andrea Leone/istockphoto.com; p. 10: Robert & Linda Mostyn; Eye
Ubiquitous/Corbis; p. 11: Kean Collection/Getty Images; p. 13: Eliza Snow/istockphoto.com;
p. 14: Kiyoshi Takahase/istockphoto.com; p. 15: Sheila Terry/Science Photo Library; p. 16:
Gary Allard/istockphoto.com; p. 18: Corbis; p. 21: Edward Parker/EASI-Images/cfwimages.com;
p. 24: Hulton Archive/Getty images; p. 25: ESA; p. 26: Warren Gretz/NREL; p. 30: ETH Zurich/
Pac-Car II; p. 33: Edward Parker/EASI-Images/cfwimages.com; p. 34: Roger Whiteway/
istockphoto.com; p. 35: Rob Bowden/EASI-Images/cfwimages.com; p. 36: The Brown Reference
Group; p. 37: Imagno/Getty Images; p. 40: NASA/MODIS Land Rapid Response Team, Jeff
Schmaltz; p. 42: Don F. Figer (UCLA)/NASA; p. 43: NASA; p. 44: Nebraska Soybean Board/NREL

Library of Congress Cataloging-in-Publication Data

Solway, Andrew.
  Energy / Andrew Solway. -- 1st ed.
      p. cm. -- (Exploring Physical Science)
  Includes index.
  ISBN-13: 978-1-4042-3748-3 (library binding)
  ISBN-10: 1-4042-3748-8 (library binding)
  1. Power resources--Juvenile literature. I. Title.
  TJ163.23.S685 2007
  621.042--dc22
                                        2006036704

Manufactured in China

Contents

CHAPTER 1

What is energy?

What would a world without energy be like? If there was a power outage to your house, the lights would not work, the TV would be blank, and if you used an electric stove, you would not be able to cook. If your car ran out of fuel, the engine would have no energy to make it work, and the car would not move. Without energy from food, animals cannot survive, and without energy from sunlight, plants cannot grow. A world without energy would be cold, dark, still, and lifeless.

So what *is* energy?

We have seen that without energy, nothing happens. So one way of describing energy is to say that it is the ability to make things happen. When electrical energy flows through the wiring in a house, the lights work, the television comes on, and the stove heats up. If the car has a full tank of fuel, you can travel for many miles without stopping. Animals that have eaten have the energy to survive and look for more food. Plants that get regular sunlight grow and produce flowers and fruit.

 AMAZING FACTS

World's biggest power outage

The power outage that probably affected more people than any other happened on August 14, 2003. A problem with a power company in Canada caused a blackout across the East Coast and Canada, affecting more than 50 million people. Traffic lights failed, underground railroads stopped, and people were trapped in elevators. In New York City, millions of people had to walk home, and some who lived too far away ended up sleeping on the streets for the night.

Another way of describing energy is that it is the capacity to do work. **Work** can mean all kinds of things, from switching on a light bulb, to growing a flower. This definition of energy is not much different from the first one, but as we will see later in the book, it is helpful when we want to measure energy.

A world of energy

In this book, we will look at different types of energy. We will look at how energy can move from place to place, and how it changes from one form to another. We will see how living things depend on the Sun's energy. Energy cannot be created or destroyed—so why are people worried that our energy might run out? There is always the same amount of energy before and after it changes form, so why do we talk about wasting energy? Keep reading to find the answers.

A large city uses an enormous amount of energy just to keep the streets and buildings lit at night.

CHAPTER 2

Adaptable energy

Energy comes in a bewildering variety of forms. Light, heat, and even sound are all forms of energy. Electricity is a very versatile kind of energy—we use it for all kinds of purposes. Anything that is moving has energy, including things like the wind (moving air) and waves (moving water). The energy of movement is called **kinetic energy**.

Potential energy

Things do not have to be hot, or moving, or making a noise to have energy. They could have potential energy. This is the energy that is not actually making something happen right now, but it could do at any moment. For instance, a person on a high diving board could be perfectly still and quiet, but they have the potential to dive or jump into the water below.

In a few seconds, this diver will be rushing downward toward the pool with a large amount of kinetic energy.

Water held in a **reservoir** by a dam also has potential energy. The water in the reservoir is still and quiet. But if we open the **sluice gates**, water rushes down tunnels and pipes until it reaches a water turbine (see page 25). By this time, it has enough kinetic energy to be able to turn the water turbine.

The potential energy of a diver or the water in a reservoir comes from gravity. The diver is supported against the pull of gravity by the diving board, and the water is held back by the dam. When the diver goes off the board, or the sluice gates open, gravity is free to act and the diver (or water) begins to fall.

Chemical energy

Another kind of energy is the energy that a car gets from its fuel, or that we can get from a fire. These types of energy come from burning, which is a chemical reaction. The energy that we get from our food is also a chemical reaction. These kinds of energy are known as **chemical energy**. Chemical energy is stored in a fuel or other chemical, ready to be converted into heat, light, or some other form of energy.

 HIGH-OCTANE FUEL

Gasoline and diesel are good fuels because they contain more energy per gallon than other fuels, as this table shows.

Fuel type	Energy megajoules (million **joules**) per gallon
Diesel	155.0
Gasoline	121.28
LPG (liquified petroleum gas)	83.98
Ethanol (alcohol)	74.24
Methanol	55.22

Energy transfer

Moving energy from one place to another, or from one object to another, is known as an **energy transfer**. Sometimes energy transfers are very useful to us, but at other times we want to stop them from happening.

One of the most useful things about electricity is that it is a form of energy that we can easily move. Overhead and underground cables carry electricity from power stations to homes, stores, offices, and factories over a large area, while smaller wires carry electricity to different parts of a house or other building.

Sound is another kind of energy that can travel. When we talk to each other, for instance, we are transferring sound energy from one place to another. A lion's roar or an elephant's low rumble can be heard for several miles, and the "songs" of some whales can travel hundreds of miles through the water.

 AMANING FACTS

Well-traveled light

Two galaxies that were discovered in 2004 are the most distant we know of. Both galaxies are 13 billion light years or more from Earth. This means that the light energy from these galaxies has taken 13 billion years to reach us. In one year, light travels 5.9 trillion miles, or 9.5 trillion kilometers, so the light from these galaxies has traveled 76.7 billion trillion miles, or 123.5 billion trillion kilometers.

The galaxy in this photograph, Messier 81, is 12 million light years away.

The best way of moving energy over really long distances is as light or some other form of **electromagnetic radiation** (such as radio waves, microwaves, or X-rays). Light from the Sun travels about 93 million miles (150 million kilometers) to pour energy on Earth. Without this energy, we would not be able to see, and plants would not be able to make their own food. Heat from the Sun is also a type of electromagnetic radiation. Heat can also be transferred from one place to another in other ways (see pages 18/19).

Kinetic energy is movement energy, so it obviously moves from place to place. But kinetic energy can also be transferred from one object to another. For instance, when you kick a soccer ball, you transfer kinetic energy from your foot to the ball, but in tennis and baseball you transfer energy to the ball from a racket or bat.

In baseball, the energy from the batter's swing is transferred from the bat to the ball.

Transforming energy

When a diver jumps from a diving board, or the **sluice gates** are opened on a dam, the potential energy of the diver or the **reservoir** is changed into another kind of energy—kinetic energy. Energy transformations are central to the many ways that we make use of energy. Electrical energy, for example, has to be transformed into some other kind of energy in order for us to use it. Light bulbs turn electrical energy into light, electric heaters and stoves turn electrical energy into heat, motors turn electricity into movement, and loudspeakers turn it into sound. Other devices work the other way, turning some other kind of energy into electrical energy. A microphone, for instance, turns sounds into electrical signals.

Many machines involve more than one energy transformation. For instance, in a car, chemical energy (the fuel) is converted in the engine into heat (the fuel burns). The heat is then used to drive the engine and make the car move, so the heat energy is converted into kinetic energy.

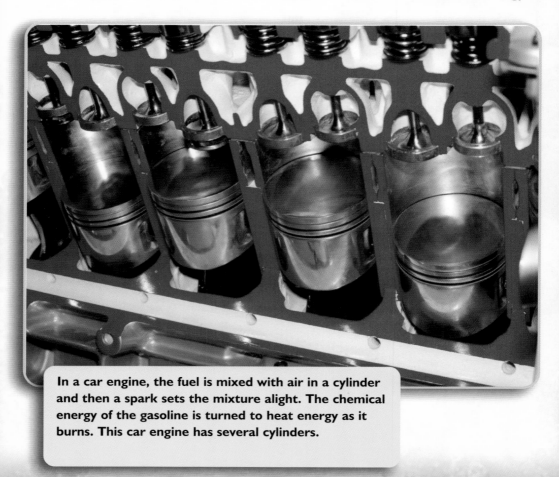

In a car engine, the fuel is mixed with air in a cylinder and then a spark sets the mixture alight. The chemical energy of the gasoline is turned to heat energy as it burns. This car engine has several cylinders.

A swinging converter

One of the most interesting energy converters is a pendulum. Pendulums are sometimes used in clocks, because the speed of their swing stays constant.

As a pendulum swings from side to side, it is constantly transforming energy. At the top of its swing, a pendulum is still and it has no kinetic energy. However, it has maximum potential energy, because it is at the highest point in its swing. As the pendulum swings down, it gradually gathers speed, until at the bottom of its swing it is moving its fastest.

At this point, the pendulum has maximum kinetic energy but no potential energy. In each swing, the pendulum converts potential energy to kinetic energy and back again.

GREAT SCIENTISTS

Galileo's pendulum

The great Italian scientist, Galileo Galilei (1564-1642), first noticed that a pendulum had a constant time for each swing as he watched a chandelier in a cathedral. He conducted a series of experiments to show that a pendulum takes the same amount of time for each swing. He began to use pendulums as clocks, timing events by the number of swings of a pendulum. Although he did not build a working clock, Galileo did begin work on one. The first working pendulum clock was actually built in 1657, by the Dutch scientist, Christaan Huygens.

A portrait of Galileo Galilei. Although Galileo never finished building a clock, he did design one. His son built the clock after Galileo's death.

Measuring energy

One of the definitions of energy at the start of the book was that it is "the capacity to do work." The advantage of this way of thinking about energy is that we can use a pre-existing scientific definition of work. This means that work, and therefore energy, can be measured. Work is the force needed to move an object multiplied by the distance it moves:

$$work = force \times distance$$

The work done (the energy involved) is measured in units called **joules (J)**. One joule is the work done when a force of 1 **newton** (N) is moved 1 meter (just over a yard).

 GREAT EXPERIMENTS

James Joule

The unit of energy is named after the English scientist, James Joule (1818-1889). Joule showed that mechanical work (for instance, turning a wheel or moving a weight) can be converted directly into heat. For years, scientists were not convinced, so Joule designed many experiments to demonstrate that he was correct. His most effective experiment was one in which he placed paddle wheels in an **insulated** barrel full of water, and made them turn by attaching them to a falling weight. By careful measurement of the temperature before and after the experiment, he showed that the mechanical work of turning the paddles had heated up the water.

Sometimes energy is measured in other units. For instance, people often talk about the number of calories in the food they eat, and calories (cal) are a measure of energy. One calorie is equal to about 4.2 joules. An average girl from 11 to 14 years old needs to eat about 1,850 **kilocalories** (kcal) or 7,745 **kilojoules** (kJ) of food a day to keep healthy, and a boy needs slightly more—2,220 kcal, or 9,259 kJ, per day.

Athletes use large amounts of energy during training and in races. A top athlete may need to eat 4,000-5,000 kcal (16,740-20,930 kJ) or more per day in order to stay healthy.

Energy and power

In ordinary speech, people often use the words "energy" and "power" almost interchangeably, but in science the words have different meanings. If energy is the amount of work needed to do a task, power is the amount of energy used in a certain amount of time to do the task. If energy is measured in joules and time is measured in seconds, the unit of power is **watts (W)**. For instance, if you use a force of 10 newtons to move an object 33 feet (10 meters), it will take 100 joules of energy. If you move the object in 10 seconds, you are using a power of 10 watts (10 joules per second). If you move the object in 1 second, you use 100 watts of power.

 ## WATTS AND LIGHT BULBS

The power of the light bulbs in your house is usually measured in watts. The most common bulbs are 40, 60, and 100 watts. A 100-watt bulb uses 100 joules of electrical energy every second. Energy-saving bulbs cost more than "normal" bulbs, but they use less power. A 20W energy-saving bulb is brighter than a 100W normal bulb, but it uses a fifth of the energy.

CHAPTER 3

Heat energy

Many scientists thought that heat was a substance until well into the nineteenth century. Today, we know that heat is a form of energy. Energy is the ability to do work, and heat does lots of work for us. Heat cooks food for us and warms our homes. Heat makes car engines work, and most power stations use heat to produce electricity. Warm-blooded animals, such as mammals and birds, generate heat in their bodies so that they can stay active in cold weather.

Heat is a form of kinetic energy, because it is produced by movement. How hot a substance is relates to the amount of movement in the tiny particles (**atoms** and **molecules**) that make up all substances.

Warm-blooded animals must use extra energy to keep their bodies warm. This is particularly difficult for small animals like this hummingbird. They must eat constantly to survive.

 GREAT SCIENTISTS

Antoine Lavoisier

In his book *The Elements of Chemistry* (1787), the French chemist, Antoine Lavoisier, listed 32 substances that he considered to be elements (substances that could not be broken down further into simpler substances). One of these "elements" was a substance that he called caloric. We know it better as heat. It took another century to prove that heat was not a substance, but a form of energy instead.

Rumford's boring barrels

The person who first began to understand the nature of heat was Benjamin Thompson (later Count Rumford). In the 1790s, Thompson was supervising work in a factory making cannons. He observed that when the insides of the cannon were being bored (smoothed by turning a special tool inside the barrel), a great deal of heat was generated. He conducted a series of experiments to measure the heat produced by the boring process.

Rumford thought that his experiments proved that the heat was being generated by the motion of the boring tool in the cannon barrel (today, we would say that the heat was the result of **friction** between the barrel and the boring tool). However, other scientists of the time were not convinced. The idea of heat as a substance persisted until Joule proved the connection between work and heat in the mid-nineteenth century (see page 12).

This illustration shows Rumford demonstrating how heat is created when boring a cannon.

The particles in a solid do not have much space to move. They vibrate back and forth around a central point. As the temperature of a solid rises, these vibrations get bigger and bigger until the solid melts and becomes liquid. In a liquid, particles have more freedom to move, and heating makes the particles move faster until the liquid turns into a gas. In a gas, the particles can move in any direction. The particles in a hot gas move faster than those in a cold gas.

Heat and temperature

Heat and temperature are not the same thing. The amount of heat in an object is the total heat energy of all the particles in the object. The temperature, on the other hand, is a measure of the average energy of the particles. There are plenty of examples of this all around us. The glowing **filament** in a light bulb has a high temperature, but it does not have much total heat. A bath full of hot water is at a much lower temperature, but it contains far more total heat.

Heat flow

If you get a phone call just as you finish making a cup of hot chocolate, you might forget about your drink. When you remember it an hour later, the chocolate will no longer be hot. This is an example of a general rule about heat—heat flows from areas of high temperature to areas of low temperature. The hot chocolate was originally at a higher temperature than its surroundings, but gradually it cools as heat flows from the hot drink into the surroundings.

Although the hot chocolate is hotter than its surroundings, it has much less heat overall than the surroundings. The heat energy from the hot chocolate is not enough to make the room significantly warmer. If you put a hot water bottle in your bed, the situation is different. Heat flows from the hot water bottle, which is at a higher temperature, to the bedclothes, which are at a lower temperature. However, there is more heat energy in the hot water bottle, and a bed is a smaller space than a room. As the hot water bottle cools down, the temperature of the bed gets higher. Eventually, the hot water bottle and the bed reach the same temperature, and the flow of heat stops.

A mug of hot tea will eventually become cold as the heat from the mug flows to the room; however, the total heat of the mug is not enough to warm the room around it.

AMAZING FACTS

Highs and lows

There is no upper limit to the temperature a substance can reach. The surface of the Sun has a temperature of about 9,900°F (5,500°C), but the core (center) has a temperature of 59-61 million °F (15-16 million °C). Other stars are considerably hotter than the Sun, and other objects in space have even higher temperatures. However, there is a lower limit to temperature. **Absolute zero** is the lowest temperature that a substance can reach, when the movement of its particles is at the absolute minimum. The temperature of absolute zero is -459.67°F, or -273.16°C.

The temperature scale ranges from absolute zero to millions of degrees.

59-61 million °F
(15-16 million °C)
core of Sun

9,900°F (5,500°C)
surface of Sun

4,532°F (2,500°C)
light bulb filament

3,632°F (2,000°C)
gas flame

2,795°F (1,535°C)
iron melts

212°F (100°C)
water boils

98.6°F (37°C)
human body

32°F (0°C)
water freezes

-0.4°F (-18°C)
frozen food

-328°F (-200°C)
liquid oxygen

-459.67°F (-273.16°C)
absolute zero

Types of heat flow

Heat flows from place to place in several different ways. First, think about a spoon in a cup of hot chocolate. At first, the handle sticking out of the drink is cool, but after a few minutes, it is as hot as the rest of the spoon. Heat has flowed along the spoon by a process called **conduction**. Hot particles in one part of the solid pass on some of their heat energy to the particles close to them. These particles pass on energy to the particles close to them, and so on.

Conductors and insulators

Not all materials conduct heat in the same way. A plastic spoon standing in a hot drink takes much longer to heat up than a metal one. Most metals are good conductors of heat. This makes metals good for the bodies of saucepans, but not so good for the handles. Instead, plastic, rubber, and wood are examples of poor heat conductors, or insulators.

Polar bears have such good insulation that they sometimes get too hot! In addition to their thick fur, they have an insulating layer of blubber (fat), which keeps them warm in the water as well as on land.

Convection

When we heat a pan of water, heat spreads through the water by a different process, known as **convection**. The water at the base of the pan is heated first. Warm water is less dense (or lighter) than cold water, so the heated water rises. Colder water then flows in to replace it. The result is a current, known as a convection current, in which the warmer water at the bottom of the pan is constantly being replaced by colder water from above. Something similar happens when any fluid (liquid or gas) is heated.

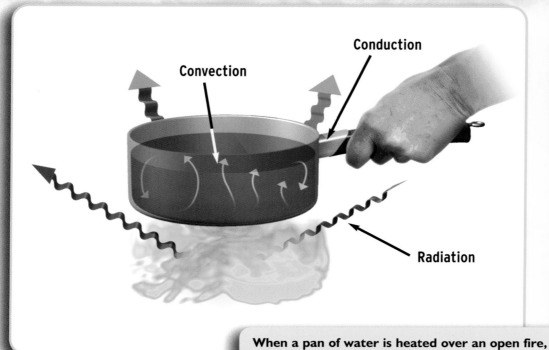

Convection

Conduction

Radiation

When a pan of water is heated over an open fire, all three kinds of heat transfer happen at the same time. Heat is conducted from the body of the pan along the handle. Convection carries heat around the water in the pan. Finally, heat radiates from the fire.

Radiation

Heat cannot travel through space by conduction or convection. Heat from the Sun reaches us by a third process, known as radiation. Heat radiation is a kind of **electromagnetic radiation** (see page 9), known as **infrared** radiation. Like light, infrared radiation travels incredibly quickly—it takes just 8 minutes for heat from the Sun to reach Earth. Many hot objects on Earth, such as the burners on a stove, also radiate heat.

 HEAT FROM THE STARS

Distant stars and galaxies produce infrared radiation just like the Sun, but it is hard to detect from Earth. The Spitzer Space Telescope solves this problem by being positioned far out in space. The telescope is shielded from the heat of the Sun, and its instruments are cooled to almost **absolute zero**. This enables it to pick up very faint infrared signals from space.

CHAPTER 4

Energy resources

In the modern world, we use energy for almost everything we do. Most of this energy comes from what we call energy resources. Between getting up in the morning and arriving at school, you probably use all kinds of energy resources. If you have a shower in the morning, the water is probably heated by electrical energy. If it is a cold day, the heating will be on. The heat energy could come from oil, gas, coal, wood, or electricity. Any lights you switch on will use electricity, as will the radio or TV. If you go to school in a car or a bus, it will need energy from gasoline or diesel fuel. Electricity, oil, fuel, gas, coal, and wood are just some of the energy resources that we rely on every day.

The pie chart shows world electricity production in 2003. Over 85 percent of the world's electricity was produced using coal, oil, and natural gas.

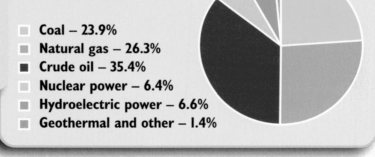

World fuel consumption

- Coal – 23.9%
- Natural gas – 26.3%
- Crude oil – 35.4%
- Nuclear power – 6.4%
- Hydroelectric power – 6.6%
- Geothermal and other – 1.4%

 MEASURING THE ENERGY IN FUELS

The best way to find out how much energy there is in a particular fuel is to burn some. However, it is difficult to measure energy directly from burning. Instead, scientists burn a measured amount of fuel under carefully controlled conditions, and use it to heat water. By measuring the temperature of the water before and after burning the fuel, and knowing the volume of the water, it is possible to work out how much heat energy the fuel produced.

Energy from fuels

Oil, gas, wood, gasoline, and diesel are all different types of fuel. We have seen already that fuels are a type of chemical energy, and that we get energy from fuels by combustion (burning). Combustion is a chemical reaction that releases heat energy. We can use this heat directly, for instance, to heat a house or other building. We can also use the heat to generate another kind of energy. In a car or other vehicle, the heat energy is converted into kinetic energy (movement). The other major way we use fuels is to generate electricity.

Electricity from fuels

Electricity is a very convenient kind of energy. It is also a clean form of energy—when things run on electricity, no smoke or fumes are created. This is why we use it in so many ways. However, electricity has to be generated somehow. The main way this is done is by burning some kind of fuel, usually oil, coal, or natural gas. The fuel is burned in a furnace, which heats water to make steam. The steam is pushed at high pressure through a machine called a steam turbine, which spins at high speed. The steam turbine is used to turn a generator, which produces electricity.

Cooling towers pour out steam and fumes from a coal-burning power station.

Fossil fuels

Coal, oil, and natural gas are collectively known as **fossil fuels**. This is because these materials were formed from the remains of plants and animals that lived hundreds of millions of years ago. Fossil fuels took millions of years to form. Although large amounts are found in underground rocks and occasionally at the surface, supplies of fossil fuels are limited. What is more, once they have been used up, these fuels cannot be replaced. This situation is worrying, because we rely so heavily on fossil fuels for energy.

How fossil fuels formed

Most of our coal deposits formed during the Carboniferous period. This was between 290 and 354 million years ago, at least 40 million years before dinosaurs existed. During the Carboniferous period, large parts of Earth were covered by vast, swampy forests. The trees and other plants in these forests rotted very slowly after they died. Over thousands of years they formed a layer of spongy material called **peat**. Gradually, the peat became buried under other rocks, which squashed down the peat layer. After years under pressure, the soft peat hardened into coal.

As with coal deposits, most of our oil and gas supplies formed over 300 million years ago. However, oil and gas formed in the sea rather than in forests. The seas swarmed with microscopic plants and animals known as **plankton**. When the plankton died, they fell to the sea bed. A layer of plankton, mixed with mud, slowly built up over the years. Later, these remains were buried, squashed, and also heated. The combination of pressure and heating slowly turned the mixture into oil or gas, depending on the temperature (gas formed at higher temperatures than oil).

 AMAZING FACTS

Prehistoric gas

Research carried out in 2003 showed that about 98.16 tons of ancient plant and animal material goes to make one gallon of oil. So to fill the 18-gallon tank of a typical family car takes the equivalent of 5,890 tons of prehistoric plants.

The oil and gas were lighter than the surrounding rocks, so slowly they filtered upward through the rocks above them. In some places, the oil or gas reached the surface. In other places, the oil or gas became trapped under a layer of **impermeable** rock that they could not filter through. This is how the oil and gas deposits we find today were formed.

COAL, OIL, AND GAS

How oil and gas were formed (top right-hand steps). 1) Oil and gas begin as tiny sea creatures that swarm in the waters. 2) As they die, they sink to the seabed. 3) The layer of dead sea creatures is buried. As it is buried deeper and gets hot, the layer turns to oil and gas. 4) Oil and gas slowly rise up through the tiny pores in the rock. 5) A layer of dense rock does not let oil and gas pass through and it becomes trapped.

How coal was formed (lower left-hand steps). 6) About 1,300 million years ago, large areas of swampy forest covered the Earth. 7) As the trees died, they were buried under a layer of mud and sand. 8) As more material built up above, the layer of rotted plant material was squashed. 9) Further pressure and heat in the earth turned the plant material into coal.

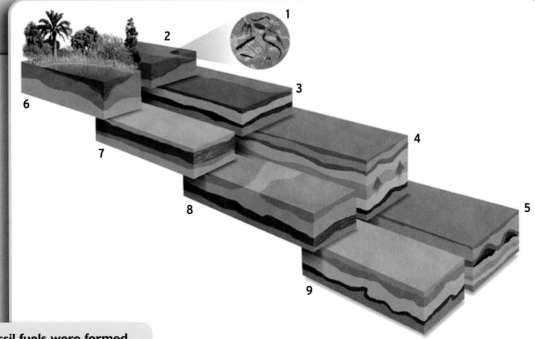

How fossil fuels were formed.

Fossil fuel alternatives

We produce so much energy using fossil fuels that they will be hard to replace. However, there are good reasons to look for alternative energy resources. As we have seen, fossil fuels are not renewable and will eventually run out. Another problem is that burning fossil fuels releases polluting gases. Burning fossil fuels also produces large amounts of carbon dioxide, a gas that is a major cause of **global warming**.

Nuclear power

Nuclear power is the most widely used form of energy after fossil fuels. As in a fossil fuel power station, a nuclear power station produces heat to make steam, which powers a steam turbine. However, the heat is produced in a nuclear reaction, in which **atoms** of the **radioactive** metal uranium are split in two, with the release of large amounts of energy. This is called a **nuclear reaction**, because it involves the nucleus (central part) of the atom. Nuclear power stations produce large amounts of energy using only small amounts of fuel. However, they are expensive to build, and an accident can cause the release of large amounts of radioactivity.

AMAZING FACTS

The first nuclear reactor

In 1942, the Italian physicist, Enrico Fermi, directed the building of the first-ever nuclear reactor, in an old sports hall at Chicago University. The reactor was called a "nuclear pile," because it was literally a carefully stacked pile of carbon blocks and small pellets of uranium.

A photograph of Enrico Fermi (1901-1954), taken around the time he built his "nuclear pile."

Hydroelectric power

Hydroelectric power is another form of energy that is widely used. The energy to turn the electric generators comes from water held back behind a large dam. Where there are suitable rivers, hydroelectric power can produce cheap electricity without pollution. However, dams can flood large areas of productive land, and they can have a bad effect on agriculture and fishing downstream of the dam.

The Three Gorges Dam on the Yangtze River in China is the largest-ever hydroelectric project. At full power, the dam will produce 18 billion **watts** of power. Over a million people have had to move from their homes to make space for the **reservoir**.

Wind power

Windmills have been used for thousands of years to pump water and grind cereals into flour. Today, propeller-style wind generators are increasingly used to produce electricity. They are most effective in windy locations, such as high ground, coastal areas, and offshore.

Single wind generators do not produce large amounts of power, so they are often grouped together in "wind farms." In the long run, wind is a reliable source of energy, but there are large variations in the amount of wind day by day. Wind farms can also be noisy, and many people dislike the way they look.

Biomass and biofuels

Biomass is any material that comes from living things. At its simplest, biomass energy is a power station using wood instead of fossil fuels. Plant and animal materials other than wood are not good fuels when they are used directly. However, crops, such as corn and sugar beet, can be turned into useful fuels, such as ethanol (alcohol) and biodiesel. Also, a wide range of biomass materials, including agricultural waste and animal dung, can be converted into gas. This is done by **fermenting** with **bacteria** or by heating under special conditions. Biomass and biofuels are often used for CHP (combined heat and power) generation. In a CHP power plant, "waste" heat produced when generating electricity is used to heat local buildings.

This power station in Burlington, Vermont, is a biomass gasifier. Here wood chips are turned into electricity.

Solar power

The Sun is an inexhaustible energy source that is available every day. However, hardly any power stations have been built to use solar power, because no cheap, effective way has been found to harness the Sun's power on a large scale. However, many homeowners have solar cells, which convert sunlight directly into electricity, on the roof of their house. Solar cells are also used to power a wide range of electrical devices, from calculators to the International Space Station.

Other energy resources

Other energy resources that are used in a limited way for power generation are the power of the waves and tides, and geothermal energy (heat energy from underground). Deep below Earth's surface, the rocks are so hot that they are almost molten, and in a few places, cracks and holes in Earth's crust allow these hot rocks close to the surface, where they can be used as a source of power.

Geothermal energy is an excellent source of power in places, such as Iceland, Japan, and New Zealand, where there is an area of hot rocks fairly close to the surface. However, there are very few good sites for geothermal power.

Early tidal power stations involved building a long barrage or barrier across a river or estuary, and used the power of the tide to drive turbines in the barrier. This kind of power station was expensive to build, and there were only a few suitable sites. More recent tidal power designs are cheaper and can be built in many more places, but so far, the ideas are untested. Similarly, there has been much work on developing practical ideas for wave-powered generators, but so far, no large, wave-powered power stations exist.

 COMPARING FUEL RESOURCES

Resource	Advantages	Disadvantages	Renewable?
Fossil fuels	• Generate lots of power cheaply • Easy to transport • Modern power stations efficient	• Produce pollution • Produce carbon dioxide • Coal mining difficult and dangerous • Mining damages landscape	No
Nuclear power	• Costs about same as fossil fuels • High energy from a small amount • No air pollution • No carbon dioxide emissions	• Waste very dangerous • High costs to ensure safety • An accident can release huge amounts of **radioactivity**	No
Hydroelectricity	• Energy almost free once dam is built • Reliable, constant energy source • No waste or pollution • Dam can be used for irrigating crops	• Dams expensive to build • Causes flooding upstream • Can affect wildlife and agriculture downstream	Yes
Wind power	• Free once generators are built • No pollution or waste • Land nearby can be farmed • Good for remote areas	• Intermittent source of energy • Low energy output • Only suitable for some locations • Can be noisy	Yes
Biomass	• Fuels usually cheap • Can use up waste materials • Does not increase carbon dioxide	• Can be difficult to get enough • Burning produces carbon dioxide and some pollutants	Yes
Solar power	• Free source of energy • Good for remote locations or warm countries • Can be used on a small scale	• Power stations are expensive • Does not work at night • Unreliable except in sunny places	Yes

CHAPTER 5

Energy savings and efficiency

Imagine you are cycling down a long, flat road. As you cycle, you are turning chemical energy from your muscles into kinetic energy (movement of the bike). At some point you decide to stop pedaling. The bike slows down, and soon you stop. What happened to all that energy you put into the bike? It seems to have disappeared. But as we will see, the energy has just changed into another form.

Friction and air resistance

When you cycle along an open road, it seems that there is nothing to hold you back. However, there is a force trying to stop you all the time. This force is **friction**. Friction between the road and the bike tires gives you grip and stops the bike from slipping. However, this friction also slows you down. There is friction in the wheel bearings, too, even though they are greased to make them move freely.

As you cycle, you feel a wind on your face, even though there is no wind when you stop. The wind is produced by another kind of friction called **air resistance**. If you wade through water, you can feel how the water resists your progress. Air is thinner than water, but it still offers some resistance as you move through it, and you feel this resistance as wind.

 DANGEROUS BRAKES

Most bikes have rubber or plastic brake blocks that press against the wheel rim to slow down or stop. This design has the disadvantage that the rims get hot through friction with the brake pads. On a heavily loaded bike in a hilly area, constant braking can heat the rims so much that the inner tube on the tire expands, and sometimes bursts.

No energy lost

Friction and air resistance are the main forces that slow the bike down when you stop pedaling. As they act, the bike loses its kinetic energy. However, the energy does not just disappear. Most of the kinetic energy transforms into heat, as the bearings, the bicycle tires, and the road are all warmed up by friction. A small amount of energy transforms into sound—the rumbling sound of the tires on the road. None of the energy is actually lost. In fact, it is a general law of physics that energy is never made or destroyed. This is known as the law of conservation of energy.

How a cyclist on a flat road loses energy. If the rider is cycling into a headwind, the air resistance will be greater, and he or she will lose energy more quickly.

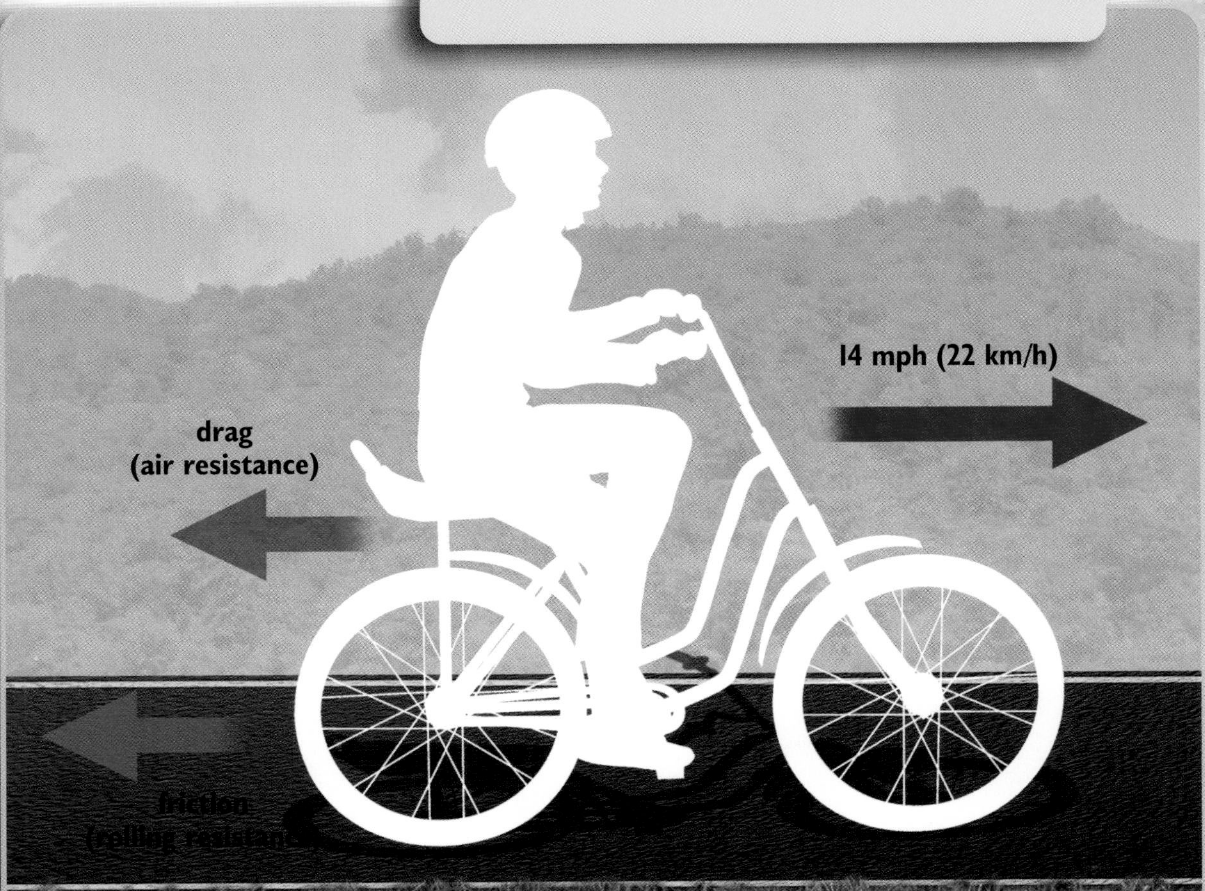

14 mph (22 km/h)

drag
(air resistance)

friction
(rolling resistance)

"Wasted" energy

If you had a bike with rusty wheel bearings, it would be much harder to pedal, and the bike would slow down more quickly when you stopped pedaling. Much of the energy you used for pedaling would be lost. It would go toward heating up the bearings, rather than moving the bike.

In any kind of process, only some of the energy is converted into useful work. The rest of the energy is "wasted," often becoming heat energy. The percentage of energy that is converted into useful work is known as the efficiency of the process. A bicycle is very efficient. Up to 99 percent of the energy you use pressing down on the pedals is converted into movement of the bike on the road.

AMAZING FACTS

Less power than a light bulb

Probably the world's most fuel-efficient vehicle is a car built by a team of designers at the Federal Institute of Technology in Zurich, Switzerland. In 2005, their hydrogen-powered vehicle managed a fuel consumption of 16,486 miles per gallon (5,835 kilometers per liter) of fuel. The power needed to keep it going is less than that of most conventional light bulbs.

In 2005, PAC-Car II set a fuel efficiency record of 16,486 miles per gallon. The car was powered by electricity, produced by a hydrogen fuel cell.

Improving efficiency

No other machines are as efficient as bicycles. Machines that have an engine of some kind—everything from lawnmowers to rockets—have a maximum energy efficiency of around 68 percent. This is to do with the nature of engines. They must produce some heat, or they don't work, and that heat is "waste" energy.

Most conventional power stations have a much lower efficiency than 68 percent. An average fossil fuel power station has an efficiency of around 35 percent, although more recent gas-powered stations can be up to 60 percent efficient. Most efficient of all are CHP (combined heat and power) power stations. Because they use the "waste" heat as well as producing electricity, the efficiency of a CHP plant can reach 70-80 percent.

Some methods of power generation do not involve using engines. Large **hydroelectric power** plants have efficiencies of between 70 and 90 percent. Wind turbines can reach efficiencies of 60 percent, but solar panels have an efficiency of only 8-15 percent. However, in these kinds of technology, where the energy is "free," efficiency is less important than the cost of producing the electricity.

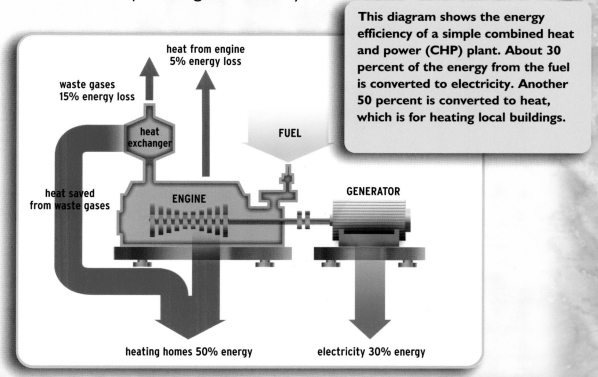

This diagram shows the energy efficiency of a simple combined heat and power (CHP) plant. About 30 percent of the energy from the fuel is converted to electricity. Another 50 percent is converted to heat, which is for heating local buildings.

heat from engine
5% energy loss

waste gases
15% energy loss

heat exchanger

FUEL

heat saved from waste gases

ENGINE

GENERATOR

heating homes 50% energy

electricity 30% energy

CHAPTER 6

Living energy

The energy you need to pedal a bike comes from your muscles, but where do your muscles get their energy from? The energy to power muscles comes from food. This can be either from eating meat or plants. Plants themselves do not eat food—they make their own using energy from sunlight.

Energy for plants

Plants make food from light through the process of **photosynthesis**. In photosynthesis, light energy from the Sun is converted into the chemical energy of foods, such as sugars.

Photosynthesis happens in a plant's leaves. The first stage involves light. Light is absorbed by colored pigments in the plant's leaves, in particular, a green pigment called chlorophyll. The light energy gained is used to make a substance called ATP (adenosine triphosphate). ATP is the main energy carrier in living things—it is like energy "money."

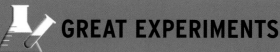 **GREAT EXPERIMENTS**

Priestley and photosynthesis

The main "waste product" of photosynthesis is oxygen. Oxygen is essential for things to burn, and animals need it to breathe. The English chemist, Joseph Priestley, showed in a series of experiments that plants produce oxygen. In one experiment, he put a sprig of mint in a sealed glass jar with a candle. He then lit the candle (by focusing sunlight on the wick). The candle went out when there was no oxygen left in the jar. Priestley then left the sealed jar for 27 days. At the end of this time he lit the candle again, and it was able to burn. Through this experiment he showed that plants produce oxygen. Soon afterward, in 1779, the Dutch-born scientist, Jan Ingenhousz, showed that plants need light in order to produce oxygen.

The second stage in photosynthesis does not need light. In this stage, carbon dioxide from the air is combined with water from the soil to make sugars. The sugars act as food for other parts of the plant. The energy needed to power this process comes from the ATP "money" made in the first stage of photosynthesis.

Energy efficiency

The efficiency of photosynthesis is very low. If you measure how much light falls on a particular area of soil in one year, then measure the weight of plants that can be grown on that area in a year, this gives an idea of the efficiency of photosynthesis. This can vary, depending on the plant, from less than 1 percent to about 3.5 percent.

A few plants, such as sugar cane, are very efficient at photosynthesis. They can turn up to 3.5 percent of the Sun's energy into plant material.

Food energy

Animals cannot turn sunlight into food as plants do. They have to eat some kind of food to get energy. No animals can feed on inorganic materials, such as rocks or air. Their food has to come from plants or from other animals.

Plant eaters

Animals that eat plants are called **herbivores**. They have a plentiful supply of food, but it can be difficult for them to get useful energy from it. This is because plants have large amounts of energy locked up in materials, such as cellulose (a stringy material found in most plants) and lignin (a tough substance found in large amounts in trees and other woody plants). Many plant eaters have found ways to digest and use the energy from cellulose. However, only a few animals (for instance, termites) are able to digest wood.

An average of only about 10 percent of the plant material that herbivores eat is turned into **animal tissue**. The rest is used up in activities, such as looking for food or finding a mate, or is lost as heat. So it takes 880 lb (400 kg) of grass to keep a 9-lb (4-kg) rabbit alive.

Herbivores, such as these fallow deer, must constantly graze on plants to keep healthy.

COMPLETING THE CYCLE

Plants and animals do not have to be living to provide a source of food. A whole range of living things, from beetles to **bacteria**, feed on dead and rotting things and on animal waste. These **decomposers**, as they are known, eventually reduce all animal and plant tissue to a few simple chemicals that enrich the soil.

Animal eaters

Animals that eat other animals are known as **carnivores**. It is easier for carnivores to digest their food and turn it into energy, but their food is harder to obtain—they have to hunt for it. As with herbivores, carnivores convert an average of about 10 percent of herbivore tissue into body tissue.

Some animals are much less efficient at converting food into body weight than others. Mammals and birds, for instance, convert only about 2 percent of their food into body weight. This is because they use a large part of their energy to keep their bodies at a constant temperature. However, animals such as reptiles and amphibians, that do not use food energy to keep their bodies warm, can convert up to 20 percent of their food into body weight.

Studies in the Serengeti plains of Africa have shown that one lion needs a population of 350 grazing animals to feed on.

CHAPTER 7

Keeping Earth going

A volcano can pour out hot lava, ash, and dust for days on end. An earthquake can destroy houses for miles around its center. An ocean storm can throw a huge tanker like a toy. Natural events like these show that Earth can produce enormous amounts of energy. Where does this energy come from?

Energy beneath Earth

The rocks beneath our feet form only a thin crust over Earth's surface. If Earth were the size of an apple, the crust would be about as thick as the apple's skin. Below the crust is a layer of very hot, partly molten rock known as the **mantle**. Below this is a third layer called the **core**, which has a fluid outer part and is solid at the center.

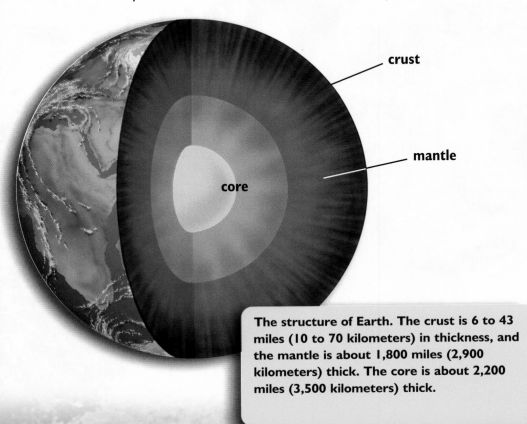

crust

mantle

core

The structure of Earth. The crust is 6 to 43 miles (10 to 70 kilometers) in thickness, and the mantle is about 1,800 miles (2,900 kilometers) thick. The core is about 2,200 miles (3,500 kilometers) thick.

The mantle is heated by **radioactive** (nuclear) reactions going on within it. Rocks that are closer to the surface are cooler than those below. The hotter rocks are less dense, and they slowly rise up through the mantle. At the same time, cooler rocks sink down deeper into the mantle. The result is huge **convection** currents, similar to those in a pan of heated water. However, these convection currents move very slowly, because the mantle rocks are like thick molasses, rather than water. It takes millions of years for rock to circulate through the mantle.

Movements on the surface

The convection movements of the mantle cause movements in Earth's crust. The crust is cracked and broken into a number of large pieces known as **plates**. These plates move along with the mantle beneath them. Plates may move toward each other, or apart, or side by side in opposite directions. Earthquakes are caused when two plates suddenly shift against each other. Volcanoes happen where hot rocks seep upward through cracks and gaps in colliding plates.

GREAT SCIENTISTS

Alfred Wegener

The German scientist, Alfred Wegener (1880-1930), first put forward the theory that Earth's crust is broken into moving plates. Wegener read research showing that similar fossils had been found on widely separated continents, and he noticed that the coasts of South America and Africa could fit together. He suggested that the continents had at one time been joined in one giant land mass. Wegener gathered much evidence to support his theory, but other scientists were not convinced. Plate tectonics, as his theory is called, was not fully accepted until the 1960s.

A photograph of the geophysicist and meteorologist, Alfred Wegener, taken around 1920.

Energy from the Sun

Apart from movement of Earth's plates, most events on Earth's surface are fueled by energy from the Sun.

About 400 million billion **joules** of energy reach us from the Sun every second. That's 32 million times more energy than the world's largest power station can produce. This energy does not fall evenly all over Earth. Because the world is spherical, and it is tilted on its axis, some parts of Earth receive much more energy than others. The area around the equator receives the most energy. This region is hotter than elsewhere. The areas around the North and South Poles receive the least of the Sun's energy, and these areas are the coldest.

We saw on page 16 that heat flows from areas of high temperature to areas of low temperature. So heat moves from hotter regions toward colder ones. This heat flow produces ocean currents and winds.

Global winds

The uneven heating of the air is the driving force behind the prevailing (main) winds on Earth. If there were no complicating factors, there would be a giant **convection** current between the equator and each of the poles. Air is warmest at the equator so it rises, and flows toward the poles at high altitudes. Near the ground, colder air flows from the poles toward the equator.

AMAZING FACTS

Trade winds

Before the twentieth century, ships crossing the oceans relied on the wind to get them to their destination. The winds blowing from east to west around the equator were known as the trade winds. Ships sailing from Europe to the Americas first sailed south, then picked up the trade winds for the passage west. On the return voyage, ships traveled in the middle latitudes, where the winds blew mainly from west to east.

In fact, the flow of air is complicated by many factors. The main one is the rotation of Earth. This breaks up the winds into three bands in each hemisphere—one close to the equator, one in the middle latitudes, and one near the poles. In each of these bands, the wind is "bent" by Earth's rotation. The winds near the equator blow roughly from the east, and in the middle latitudes, they blow roughly from the west. In the polar regions, the winds blow from the east. Over land, wind patterns are more complicated because local features, such as mountain ranges, affect the winds.

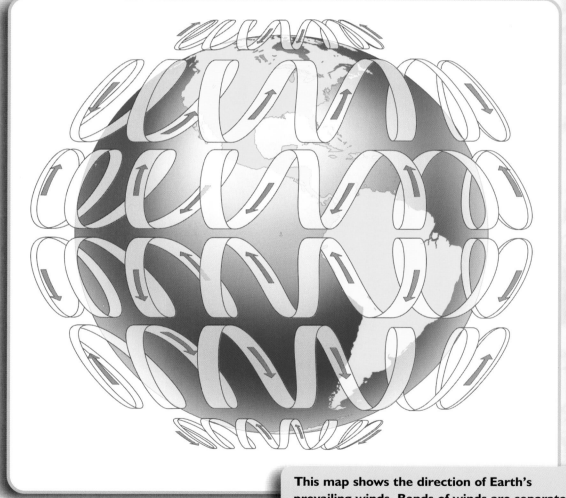

This map shows the direction of Earth's prevailing winds. Bands of winds are separated by areas where there is little wind. The windless region around the equator is called "the doldrums."

Powering the weather

The winds, the Sun, and the oceans between them are responsible for most of the weather around the world.

How warm or cold a place is depends mainly on how much sunlight it receives. Broadly, the closer a place is to the equator, the warmer its climate is.

The amount of rainfall a place receives relates to how far it is from the sea and the direction of the prevailing winds. The Sun's energy warms the oceans, and causes water from the ocean surface to evaporate (become gas) and rise into the air. Prevailing winds then carry the moist air until it is cooled in some way (for instance, by rising over high ground). As the air cools, the water in it condenses (becomes liquid). At first the water forms tiny droplets that float through the air as clouds. However, as water droplets combine and get bigger, they become too heavy to float, and they fall as rain. If it is cold enough for the water to freeze, it may fall as snow or hail instead.

AMAZING FACTS

Energetic storms

It is not always obvious that the weather involves large amounts of energy. However, there is a great deal of power in a hurricane, as can be seen from the damage it can cause. The power used to sustain the rainfall in a hurricane for one day is 600,000 billion **watts**. This is 200 times the power output of all the power stations in the world!

From a satellite high above Earth, the spiral shape of a hurricane can be seen clearly. The "eye" at the center, where there are no winds and the sky is clear, is a feature of any hurricane.

Ocean currents

Winds and uneven heating of the oceans together cause ocean currents. Heating causes water to expand, so at the equator the ocean surface is actually about 3 inches (8 centimeters) higher than at the poles. This slight difference makes the water tend to flow from the equator toward the poles. However, as with the winds, Earth's rotation has an effect on the motion, as do the prevailing winds. The result is that at the surface, the ocean currents flow in great circles, known as **gyres**, around each **ocean basin**.

Ocean currents can have a large effect on the climate of land close by. Britain and Western Europe have a much warmer climate than most other places at the same latitude because of the warming effects of the Gulf Stream, a warm current that flows across the Atlantic Ocean from the Gulf of Mexico, then runs north up the coast of Western Europe.

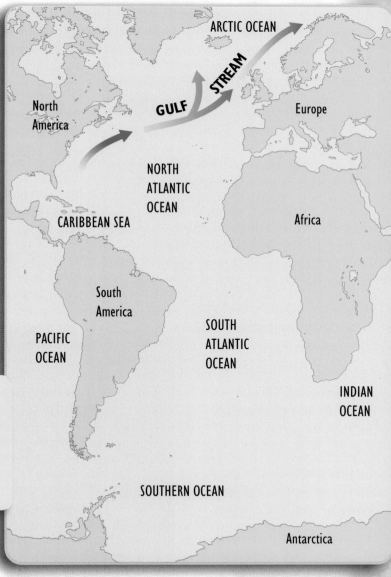

This map shows the path of the Gulf Stream, which starts in the Gulf of Mexico and runs across the Atlantic Ocean toward the coast of Western Europe.

CHAPTER 8

Energy connections

Suppose you could follow a light beam as it arrived at Earth's surface. From what we have already learned, there are many different things that could happen to the light energy. It could be absorbed by a rock, then radiate out again as **infrared** radiation (heat). It could be absorbed by a leaf, converted into chemical energy, and eventually become part of the plant. The plant could then be eaten by a herbivore, which could be eaten by a carnivore. The light beam could land on the ocean, and give some water enough energy to evaporate. Winds could then carry the moisture many miles before it falls as rain. Or the light could land on a solar cell and be converted into electricity. The electricity could be used to power a light bulb, and become light once again.

AMAZING FACTS

Dwarfing the Sun's energy

The amount of energy that a star produces is related to its brightness. The Sun is below average in terms of energy output. The brightest star in the sky, Sirius, is almost 23 times brighter than the Sun. However, Sirius is over 500,000 times farther from Earth, so it shows only as a bright pinprick in the night sky. Other stars are even brighter than Sirius, but they do not shine so brightly in our night sky, because they are even farther away. Really giant stars can be several million times brighter than the Sun.

One of the stars in the constellation of Orion is known as the Pistol Star. It is about 10 million times brighter than the Sun, making it one of the brightest stars we know of. However, it is so far away that it is too faint to see without a telescope.

Transforming the Sun's energy

The many ways that energy from sunlight can be transformed illustrate just how much we rely on the Sun's energy. We have seen that energy generated in the rocks underground powers earthquakes and volcanoes, and the force of gravity can power a downhill bike ride. However, almost every other kind of energy comes in one way or another from the Sun. The Sun's energy powers the winds, the weather, and the movements of the oceans. Plants rely on sunlight for energy, and animals and other living things get their energy directly or indirectly from plants. Eighty-five percent of the energy that humans use comes from fossil fuels, which are the remains of plants and animals made using the Sun's energy millions of years ago. Even **hydroelectricity** relies on energy from sunlight—if the Sun did not shine, all the water on Earth would be frozen as ice, rather than flow freely.

The Sun is Earth's power station. Every form of energy on Earth ultimately comes from the Sun.

Energy in the future

Human energy needs are always increasing, and our main energy source (fossil fuels) is in limited supply. So what will we do for energy in the future? There are many different ideas. Energy production from **biomass** seems likely to increase, as will the energy from renewable sources and perhaps from nuclear power. There are also newer sources of energy that might be used.

This bus in Nebraska runs on soybean biodiesel.

Fuel cells

A fuel cell is like a cross between a battery and an engine. Like an engine, it needs fuel to work (many fuel cells use hydrogen). However, a fuel cell does not burn its fuel. Instead, it uses the fuel to make electricity, like a battery. Fuel cells can produce more power than batteries, and because they run on fuel, they do not need recharging. Because they do not burn their fuel, they are more efficient than engines. A fuel cell using hydrogen as a fuel can be 80 percent efficient. Fuel cells are already used to power artificial satellites and space probes as well as remote weather stations. Most cars that can run on more than one type of fuel have fuel cells.

HYDROGEN ECONOMY

Hydrogen has a major advantage over fossil fuels—it produces only water when burned. Hydrogen can also be used to power fuel cells and make electricity. Unfortunately, at the present time, hydrogen is made mainly from natural gas, a fossil fuel. There are many other ways of making hydrogen, the most promising of which is perhaps to make it from water. The hydrogen could then be used to produce energy when it is needed. The water produced when hydrogen is used as a fuel could be collected and converted into hydrogen once again.

Solar ideas

Today, solar energy supplies very little of our total energy, but there are several ways that this contribution could increase. Solar collectors, which gather the Sun's heat and use it to heat a liquid or power an engine, combined with solar cells generating electricity, could be used much more widely on houses and other buildings. In the future, satellites in space could collect solar energy and then beam it down to Earth using **microwaves**.

The initial costs of constructing a solar power satellite currently make this form of electricity much too expensive. However, newer, low-cost ways of getting into space may soon be available, and this could make a solar power satellite practical.

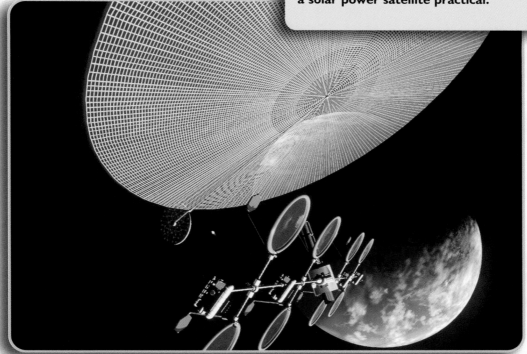

Nuclear fusion

Since the 1950s, scientists have been researching the use of **nuclear fusion** to produce energy. Nuclear fusion is the way that the Sun produces its energy. The process produces much more energy than **nuclear fission** (the way that current nuclear power stations produce energy). Furthermore, fusion does not produce dangerous **radioactive** wastes. Scientists have found ways to make fusion happen. However, so far the process uses almost as much energy as it produces. There are many problems to be solved before fusion can become a useful source of energy.

Glossary

absolute zero the lowest possible temperature, exactly -459.67°F or -273.16°C.

animal tissue group of similar cells, such as muscle.

atoms very tiny particles that make up all substances.

bacteria very tiny, simple microorganisms (microscopic creatures).

biomass any material that comes originally from living things.

convection the movement of heat by circulation of air or water currents.

electromagnetic radiation any type of radiation with similar qualities to light, such as infrared, ultraviolet, X-rays, microwaves, and radio waves.

fermenting mixing substances with microorganisms, such as bacteria or yeasts, in a warm environment with no air present.

filament in a light bulb, the filament is the very thin, tightly coiled wire that glows white-hot when the bulb is switched on.

friction a force between two objects rubbing against each other that resists the movement. Friction between two materials also generates heat.

global warming a gradual warming of Earth's climate, which has been happening for the last 150 years or so.

hydroelectric power producing electricity using flowing water.

impermeable a substance that is impermeable does not allow liquid or gas to pass through it.

infrared a kind of radiation, similar to light but invisible, which carries heat rather than light energy.

insulated protected from losing or gaining heat.

joule (J) the unit of measurement of energy. One J is the energy needed to move an object weighing 1 newton a distance of 1 meter.

kilocalorie (kcal) a unit used for measuring the amount of energy in food. A chocolate cookie contains about 525 kcal of energy.

kilojoules (kJ) One kilojoule equals one thousand joules.

megajoules a million joules (J).

microwaves a type of electromagnetic radiation similar to radio waves. The energy of microwaves can be used to heat up living tissue.

molecule a combination of two or more atoms joined together by chemical bonds.

newton (N) the unit of measurement used to measure force. On Earth, a medium-sized apple weighs about 1 N.

nuclear fission a reaction involving the nucleus of an atom, in which uranium atoms are split into smaller atoms.

nuclear fusion a reaction involving the nucleus of an atom, in which hydrogen atoms fuse (join together) to form helium atoms.

ocean basin deep sections of the ocean, divided from each other by shallower areas called midocean ridges.

radioactive a material that is radioactive gives out invisible, high-energy radiation. Radioactivity is harmful to humans.

reservoir an artificial lake made by damming a river.

sluice gates strong gates at the top of a water channel that control the flow along the channel.

watt (W) a measurement of power. One watt is the use of 1 joule of energy every second.

Further information

Books

Energy, Neil Ardley and Jack Challoner (Steck-Vaughn, 2000)

Energy (Eyewitness Science), Jack Challoner
(Dorling Kindersley Publishing, 1993)

Energy and Forces, (Young Oxford Library of Science),
Neil Ardley (Oxford University Press USA, 2003)

Energy and Resources (Sustainable Future), Paul Brown
(Franklin Watts Ltd, 2000)

Energy Projects for Young Scientists, Richard Craig Adams and
Robert Gardner (Franklin Watts Ltd, 2003)

Web sites

Due to the changing nature of Internet links,
The Rosen Publishing Group, Inc., has developed
an online list of Web sites related to the subject of
this book. This site is updated regularly. Please
use this link to access the list:
www.rosenlinks.com/ps/energy/

Index

El Joven Investi

Energía

Terry Jennings

Ilustraciones:
Karen Daws
Tudor Artists
Tony Morris

Traducción del inglés:
Pedro Barbadillo

Distributed By
LAREDO PUBLISHING CO.
22930 Lockness Ave.
Torrance, CA 90501
(800) 547-5113

Primera edición: junio 1987
Segunda edición: abril 1988
Tercera edición: agosto 1990
Cuarta edición: mayo 1992

Título original: *The Young Scientist Investigates.*
Energy.
Publicado por Oxford University Press

© Terry Jennings, 1984
© Ediciones SM, 1987
    Joaquín Turina, 39 - 28044 Madrid

ISBN: 84-348-2246-6
Depósito legal: M-15270-1992
Fotocomposición: Grafilia, SL
Impreso en España/Printed in Spain
Orymu, SA - Ruiz de Alda, 1 - Pinto (Madrid)

Comercializa: CESMA, SA - Aguacate, 25 - 28044 Madrid

Índice

Las cosas que se mueven tienen energía

Observa el dibujo. En él se ven muchas cosas en movimiento. Los niños juegan. Las gaviotas revolotean en busca de comida. El burro camina por la playa, paseando a unos niños. Al fondo circulan unos coches por la avenida. En el mar se ven unas barcas. Por el cielo cruza un avión. Todas estas cosas se mueven porque tienen energía. Las cosas al moverse consumen energía. La energía es el «motor» de las cosas.

También necesitamos energía para calentar nuestras casas en invierno y para enfriarlas en verano. Las chimeneas emplean un combustible, que desprende calor. El calor es una forma de energía. En verano utilizamos un ventilador eléctrico para refrescarnos. Para alumbrar nuestras casas utilizamos la electricidad. La electricidad es otra forma de energía.

La energía y nuestro cuerpo

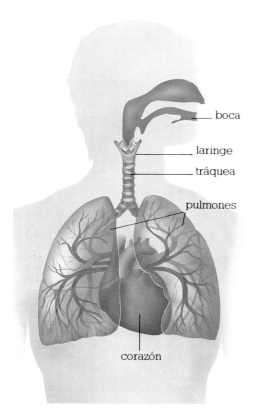

boca

laringe

tráquea

pulmones

corazón

Nosotros estamos consumiendo energía continuamente. La consumimos cuando andamos, corremos, sonreímos o hablamos. Hasta cuando estamos sentados consumimos energía. Incluso consumimos energía cuando estamos durmiendo. Cuando estamos dormidos, nuestro cuerpo consume energía para mantener en funcionamiento el corazón, los pulmones, etc. Sin embargo, consumimos mucha más energía cuando estamos despiertos. Algunas actividades, como correr, saltar o trabajar duro, consumen gran cantidad de energía.

La energía que hace que nuestro cuerpo funcione proviene de los alimentos. La energía calorífica, que mantiene el calor de nuestro cuerpo, también viene de los alimentos. Nuestro cuerpo produce energía al consumir los alimentos que comemos. Esta producción de energía tiene lugar en los músculos.

Cuando respiramos, los pulmones toman oxígeno del aire que nos rodea. El corazón manda el oxígeno, junto con la sangre, desde los pulmones hasta todos los lugares donde se necesita. El corazón manda también los alimentos transformados y disueltos en la sangre, hasta donde se precisen. En los músculos, el oxígeno se emplea para consumir los alimentos transformados, y para producir energía.

3

Realizar un trabajo

Si queremos mover alguna cosa, la tenemos que empujar o tirar de ella. Eso es trabajo. Realizamos un trabajo cuando movemos algo, empujándolo o arrastrándolo. Cuando realizas un trabajo, gastas energía. Después de realizar un gran trabajo, te sientes cansado y necesitas descansar. También sientes hambre. Comes para producir más energía.

Los animales también gastan energía al realizar un trabajo. El caballo de la foto está gastando energía al tirar del carro. Su energía proviene del alimento que come. La pala excavadora está realizando un trabajo. La energía que consume proviene del petróleo que la excavadora quema en su motor. El tren de juguete realiza un trabajo al moverse. La energía que consume proviene de la electricidad que mueve el motor de la locomotora. El coche realiza un trabajo al transportar a los pasajeros. La energía necesaria para moverse proviene de la gasolina que el coche quema en su motor.

La energía del sol

A la mayoría de la gente le gusta pasear cuando hace sol. La energía calorífica del sol nos calienta. La energía luminosa del sol nos permite ver las cosas. La energía del sol hace crecer las plantas. Las plantas usan la energía luminosa del sol para fabricarse el alimento. La energía luminosa del sol transforma el dióxido de carbono procedente del aire, el agua y las sales minerales del suelo en alimento para las plantas.

Cuando comemos algo que procede de una planta, por ejemplo una manzana, una patata, una nuez o una lechuga, obtenemos energía de ello. La energía que conseguimos de la manzana, la patata, la nuez o la lechuga procede, originalmente, del sol.

Los cerdos, las ovejas, las vacas y otros muchos animales se alimentan de plantas que consiguieron su energía del sol.

La madera proviene de los árboles. La madera puede quemarse para producir energía calorífica y energía luminosa. El árbol consiguió estas energías del sol.

Más energía del sol

Este molino de viento muele el trigo

Este molino de viento eleva el agua de un pozo

El sol calienta la tierra. La tierra calienta el aire que hay sobre ella. El aire caliente sube, y el aire más frío se desplaza para ocupar el lugar que dejó el aire caliente. Al aire en movimiento lo llamamos viento. Podemos utilizar la energía del viento para mover las aspas de un molino de viento. El molino de viento se empleaba antes para moler trigo, y en la actualidad para elevar agua y para producir electricidad. La energía necesaria para todo esto vino inicialmente del sol.

El sol calienta también el agua de los lagos, ríos y mares. El agua caliente se evapora, se convierte en vapor de agua que asciende en el aire y se enfría, formando nubes. El vapor de agua de las nubes se convierte en lluvia y cae sobre la tierra. El agua de lluvia va a parar a los arroyos y a los ríos, y éstos van a parar al mar.

Se utiliza la energía de la corriente de un río en los molinos hidráulicos. Esta energía, que mueve la rueda del molino hidráulico, vino inicialmente del sol.

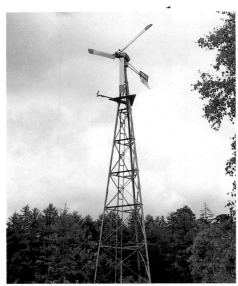

Este molino de viento produce electricidad

Molino hidráulico

Carbón

Se llama combustible a todo aquello que arde.
Al quemarse un combustible, se produce energía.

El carbón es uno de los combustibles más
importantes. El carbón se formó a partir de árboles y
otros vegetales que vivieron hace millones de años.
Esos árboles y vegetales utilizaron la energía solar
para crecer y desarrollarse. Más tarde murieron y
fueron cubiertos por barro y arena. El barro y la
arena los fueron prensando. Lentamente, el barro y
la arena se fueron transformando en rocas. El peso
de las rocas sobre aquellos árboles y demás
vegetales hizo que se fueran convirtiendo poco a
poco en carbón.

A veces encontramos fósiles de las plantas que
originaron el carbón. A veces el carbón se
encuentra cerca de la superficie de la tierra, pero
la mayor parte de las veces se encuentra a grandes
profundidades y tiene que ser extraído excavando
minas. Cuando quemamos carbón, obtenemos de él
parte de la energía solar que utilizaron los árboles y
demás vegetales hace muchísimo tiempo.

Fósil de una de las plantas que formaron
el carbón

Extracción de carbón en una mina

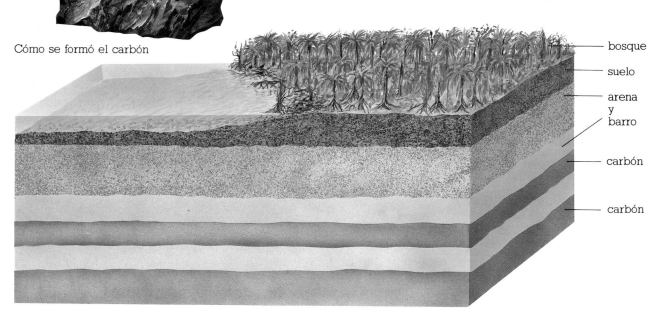

Cómo se formó el carbón

bosque

suelo

arena
y
barro

carbón

carbón

Petróleo y gas natural

Una de las plantas diminutas que dieron lugar a la formación de petróleo

Otro combustible muy importante es el petróleo. El petróleo se formó a partir de diminutas plantas y animales marinos que murieron hace millones de años. Durante su vida, esos diminutos animales y plantas marinos utilizaron la energía solar para crecer y desarrollarse. A su vez sirvieron de alimento a minúsculos animales marinos. Al morir esas plantas y animales caían al fondo del mar. Allí las cubrían el barro y la arena, que poco a poco se iban transformando en rocas. Al cabo de millones de años, aquellas plantas y animales marinos se fueron convirtiendo en gotitas de petróleo.

En algunos sitios, las rocas formaron grandes cavidades y el petróleo quedó encerrado en unos grandes lagos subterráneos. Este petróleo sale al perforar las rocas.

El gas natural es también un combustible muy importante. Se encuentra bajo tierra, como el petróleo. A veces se encuentra bajo las rocas del fondo marino.

Cuando utilizamos petróleo o gas, estamos aprovechando parte de la energía que procedió del sol hace muchísimo tiempo. Esa energía se encontraba en los cuerpos de aquellos pequeños animales y plantas que, al morir lentamente, fueron formando el petróleo y el gas natural.

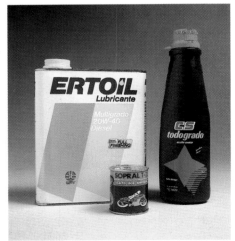
Aceite de petróleo utilizado en los motores de los coches

Corte transversal de un pozo de petróleo

Pozo de petróleo

Calor

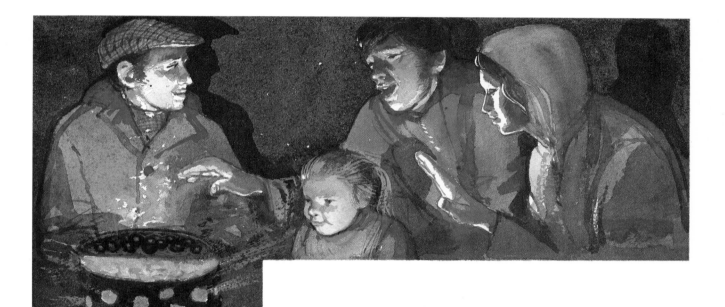

Cuentas de cristal en una olla

agua

cuentas
de cristal

la tapa
se levanta

vapor

burbujas
de aire

cuentas
de cristal

calor

El fuego nos calienta. También nos da luz. En la cara y en las manos notamos el calor que despide el fuego. El calor nos hace sentirnos a gusto. La energía calorífica proviene de la madera, del carbón o de otros combustibles, al quemarlos.

Pero el calor puede realizar también un trabajo. El calor puede hacer que algunas cosas se muevan. Puedes comprobar cómo el calor mueve algunas cosas, si pones una olla a hervir en el fuego. Antes de encender el fuego, echa un puñado de cuentas de cristal en el agua. Luego, cubre ligeramente la olla con su tapadera. Cuando el agua esté caliente, oirás cómo saltan las cuentas dentro de la olla. Puede que, incluso, la tapadera comience a subir y a bajar. El calor del fuego calienta el agua lo suficiente para transformarla en vapor de agua. Cuando el agua se convierte en vapor, aumenta el volumen y ocupa más espacio. El vapor ejerce una fuerza sobre la tapadera de la olla y la hace subir y bajar. Esta fuerza también hace que el agua burbujee y que las cuentas de cristal salten dentro de la olla.

¿Te acuerdas?

(Si no sabes las respuestas, búscalas en las páginas anteriores.)

1 ¿Qué tienen todas las cosas que se mueven?

2 ¿Qué es la energía?

3 ¿Cómo utilizamos la energía en nuestras casas?

4 ¿Cuándo gasta energía nuestro cuerpo?

5 ¿Cómo produce energía nuestro cuerpo?

6 ¿Qué les sucede a los alimentos y al oxígeno en los músculos?

7 ¿Cómo movemos algo?

8 ¿De dónde toma un caballo su energía?

9 ¿Cómo usan las plantas la energía de la luz del sol?

10 ¿De dónde proviene la energía de nuestros alimentos?

11 ¿De dónde provienen las energías calorífica y luminosa que produce la madera al arder?

12 ¿Qué sucede cuando el sol calienta la tierra?

13 Nombra tres aplicaciones de los molinos de viento.

14 ¿Qué sucede cuando el sol calienta el agua de los lagos, de los ríos y de los mares?

15 ¿Cómo podemos aprovechar la energía de las corrientes fluviales?

16 ¿Qué es un combustible?

17 ¿Cómo se formó el carbón?

18 ¿De dónde proviene la energía del carbón?

19 ¿Cómo se formó el petróleo?

20 ¿Cómo puede el calor efectuar un trabajo?

Cosas para hacer

1 **La energía de la luz solar y las plantas.** Pide permiso para colocar un ladrillo o una plancha de madera sobre el césped, durante una semana más o menos. Al cabo de ese tiempo quita el ladrillo, o la madera, y observa lo que le ha pasado al césped. ¿Qué has aprendido respecto a la luz del sol y las plantas?

2 **Usa tus músculos.** Coge una pesa de 1 kg con la mano derecha. Separa la pesa de tu cuerpo. Con la mano izquierda palpa los músculos de tu brazo derecho. Levanta la pesa lentamente. ¿Notas cómo trabajan los músculos de tu brazo? ¿Qué pasa cuando se cansan los músculos del brazo que sostiene la pesa?

Ahora deja la pesa y descansa un rato. Luego, coge otra vez la pesa y anota cuánto tiempo puedes sujetarla con el brazo extendido. Descansa de nuevo. Anota ahora el tiempo que puedes sujetar la pesa con la otra mano y el brazo extendido.

¿Con qué mano y brazo puedes sujetar más tiempo la pesa? ¿Es el brazo y la mano con la que escribes?

3 ¿A qué ritmo respiras? Pídele a un amigo que te ayude. Siéntate reposadamente en una silla y dile a tu amigo que cuente cuántas veces respiras por minuto. Es mejor realizar la prueba tres veces y calcular la media de las tres.

Averigua cuántas veces respiras por minuto, después de:

a) Haber estado quieto durante cinco minutos.
b) Haber dado una vuelta alrededor del campo de juegos *andando*.
c) Haber dado una vuelta alrededor del campo de juegos *corriendo*.
d) Haber estado dando saltos durante dos minutos.

Refleja los resultados en un papel cuadriculado, en una gráfica.

¿Qué conclusiones sacas al ver el número de veces que respiras por minuto después de realizar estos ejercicios? ¿Cuándo respiras más agitadamente? ¿Cuándo respiras más reposadamente?

¿Qué relación puede haber entre la energía y el número de veces que respiras por minuto?

Cambia ahora con tu amigo. ¿Respira con mayor o menor ritmo que tú, después de realizar los ejercicios? ¿Es tu amigo más grande o más pequeño que tú? ¿Es mejor o peor deportista que tú?

Dile a una persona mayor que te enseñe a tomarte el pulso. ¿Cuántas pulsaciones por minuto

tienes después de realizar los diferentes ejercicios?

4 Estudio sobre comidas y bebidas. Pregunta a tus amigos qué comida y bebida prefieren en un día muy caluroso y un día muy frío. No olvides incluirte tú en el estudio.

Haz una gráfica con los resultados.

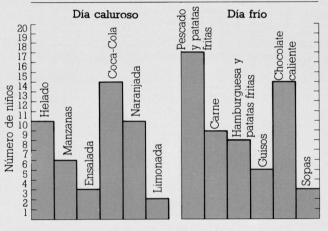

Comidas y bebidas

5 Construye una perinola. Sobre un trozo de cartulina, dibuja con un compás un círculo de unos 7 u 8 cm de diámetro. Recorta el círculo y coloréalo. Pasa el lápiz a través del centro del círculo. La cartulina debe ajustarse lo más posible al lápiz y debe quedar un poco más arriba de la punta del lápiz.

Haz girar el lápiz como una peonza. ¿Qué colores ves cuando gira el disco? ¿De dónde proviene la energía que hace girar el disco? ¿Qué hace que el disco se pare?

11

6 Molinillos de papel. Haz varios molinillos de papel. Necesitarás unos trozos cuadrados de papeles de colores, unas tijeras, unos alfileres de cabeza grande. Necesitarás también una varilla de madera de unos 30 cm de longitud y unos trocitos de una pajita de refrescos.

Realiza el trabajo con varios amigos y construid unos cuantos molinillos de papel de diferentes tamaños.

Traza con un lápiz unas líneas que unan los cuatro vértices del papel. Marca el centro del papel. Haz un corte sobre cada línea, de unas tres cuartas partes de su longitud, aproximadamente.

Dobla sobre el centro una esquina sí y otra no, y atraviesa las cuatro esquinas dobladas con un alfiler. Pasa también el alfiler a través de *un trozo* de pajita para refrescos, detrás del molinillo de papel, y clava el conjunto en la varilla de madera.

En el patio de juegos, o en el campo de deportes, correr con vuestros molinillos. ¿Giran más los molinillos si corréis más?

Si tú y tus amigos corréis a la misma velocidad, ¿giran todos los molinillos a la misma velocidad?

¿Qué molinillo gira más, el más pequeño o el más grande?

7 En una mina de carbón. Hoy, las carretillas cargadas de carbón se mueven mediante motores. Pero, hasta hace poco, las carretillas eran arrastradas por ponis. Estos caballitos pasaban toda, o parte de su vida, bajo tierra.

Escribe un relato sobre la vida de esos ponis o sobre la de los hombres que trabajaban en una mina. Titula tu relato «La vida a un kilómetro bajo tierra».

8 Maqueta de una mina de carbón. Construye una maqueta de una mina de carbón. Hazla según un corte transversal, para que pueda verse lo que sucede bajo tierra. Emplea barro o plastilina para representar las capas de carbón. Para hacer los edificios de la mina, utiliza cartón o piezas de un juego de construcción.

9 Barco de vela. Los barcos de vela utilizan la energía del viento para navegar.

Construye un barco de vela sencillo con un trozo de madera. Corta la proa del barco en forma puntiaguda.

Haz la vela con un trozo de cartulina delgada. Sujétala a un clavo largo, pasando éste por dos puntos de la vela, como ves en la figura. Clava el clavo en la cubierta del barco.

Coloca el barco en un recipiente con agua. Si se vuelca, nivélalo con un trocito de plastilina hasta que flote horizontal.

Utiliza una pajita de las de refrescos, o un pulverizador de plástico vacío, para echar aire sobre la vela. Echa el aire siempre en el centro de la vela, pero cambia de vez en cuando la posición de la vela, según distintos ángulos. ¿Cómo se mueve el barco? ¿Qué harías para que doblase a la izquierda o a la derecha?

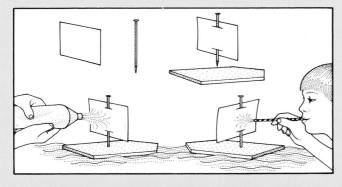

10 Cartel sobre la energía petrolífera. Consigue una hoja grande de papel, o una cartulina, para hacer un cartel. Reúne fotos o dibujos que tengan relación con el petróleo. En una de las esquinas superiores pega una foto de los animales y plantas a partir de los cuales se formó el petróleo. Traza una flecha desde esta foto hasta otra que muestre un equipo de perforación o un pozo de petróleo. Desde ésta, traza otra flecha hasta una o más fotos que muestren las muchas cosas que se pueden fabricar a partir del petróleo, o que se mueven gracias al petróleo. Escribe una o dos frases junto a cada una de las fotos. Confecciona un cartel similar sobre el carbón y las cosas que se pueden hacer a partir de él.

11 Estudio sobre la calefacción. Realiza un estudio entre los chicos de tu clase. Pregúntales si en sus casas usan electricidad, gas, petróleo, carbón, o algún otro tipo de combustible para la calefacción.

Haz una gráfica con el resultado obtenido:

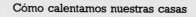

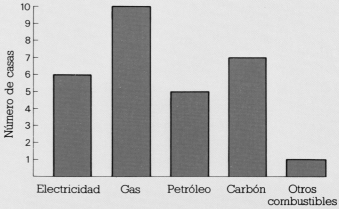

¿Qué combustible es el más corriente? ¿Por qué? Anota los motivos que te den tus compañeros.

Realiza un estudio similar para averiguar qué tipos de combustibles usan para cocinar.

12 Temperaturas. Con un termómetro, mide la temperatura del exterior de tu colegio o de tu casa. Entra luego en tu clase, o en tu casa, y mide la temperatura del interior.

Repite lo mismo durante varios días, a la misma hora.

Dibuja un gráfico que muestre dos curvas de temperatura, una para el interior y otra para el exterior. Escribe todas las razones que se te ocurran para explicar la diferencia entre las dos temperaturas.

Electricidad

Escalera mecánica eléctrica

Solemos utilizar mucho la electricidad. La usamos para iluminar las habitaciones y para cocinar los alimentos. También, para conservar los alimentos fríos y frescos, para poner en funcionamiento las máquinas y para otras muchas cosas. La electricidad es otra forma de aprovechar la energía que hay en el carbón, en el petróleo o en otros combustibles. La electricidad es limpia y fácil de usar. Sólo con dar a un interruptor, tenemos la electricidad a nuestra disposición.

La electricidad que usamos en las casas, tiendas, fábricas, etc., se produce en las centrales eléctricas. En algunas centrales eléctricas se quema carbón. El carbón, al arder, calienta el agua de unas grandes calderas y la transforma en vapor. Como vimos en la página 9, el vapor tiene un gran poder de empuje. El vapor mueve una gran rueda llamada turbina y la hace girar. La turbina, a su vez, hace girar una máquina llamada generador. Cuando el generador gira, produce electricidad.

Otras centrales eléctricas queman petróleo o gas (en vez de petróleo) para calentar el agua.

Central eléctrica que usa carbón

Central eléctrica: turbinas y generadores

14

Otras formas de producir electricidad

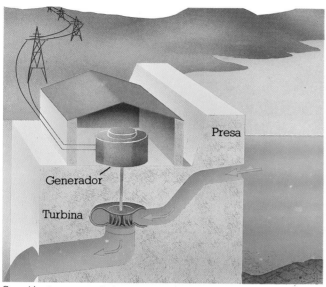

Sección transversal de una central hidroeléctrica

Presa

Generador

Turbina

Central hidroeléctrica

Central nuclear

Uranio en una central eléctrica

Hasta hace casi cien años, la gente utilizaba las corrientes de los ríos rápidos para mover los molinos y moler el trigo o el maíz. Aún hoy se ven algunos de esos molinos hidráulicos. Hoy día, se obtiene a veces la electricidad utilizando el agua para mover una rueda hidráulica especial. Esta rueda hidráulica es la turbina. El agua de un río de corriente rápida es conducida por tuberías a una central eléctrica. Allí el agua mueve las turbinas y éstas hacen girar los generadores, los cuales producen electricidad. Este tipo de central eléctrica se llama *central hidroeléctrica.* Las centrales hidroeléctricas se construyen en lugares donde hay montañas y ríos rápidos.

Las *centrales eléctricas nucleares* utilizan un mineral llamado uranio. El uranio desprende energía nuclear o atómica. La energía nuclear o atómica calienta el agua de la central eléctrica. El agua se transforma en vapor, que genera electricidad.

15

Nuevas formas de obtener energía

Cada vez utilizamos más energía en nuestras casas y en las tiendas, fábricas y oficinas. La mayor parte de la energía que usamos proviene del petróleo, del carbón y del gas. Ahora bien, en el mundo hay una cantidad *limitada* de petróleo, de carbón y de gas. Por ello los científicos están investigando nuevas formas de obtener energía.

Existen otras formas de obtener electricidad. Este gran molino de viento aprovecha la energía del viento para mover un generador, que produce electricidad. En algunos países se aprovecha la energía de las mareas de las costas para mover generadores y producir electricidad.

En algunos lugares próximos a volcanes se encuentra agua subterránea caliente. Esta agua caliente se emplea para mover máquinas en las fábricas y para la calefacción de las casas. Las astronaves utilizan la energía solar. Para ello van provistas de unas células solares que reciben la luz del sol y la convierten en electricidad.

Existen otras formas de obtener agua caliente. Estos paneles solares reciben, y absorben, el calor procedente del Sol. Cuando se calientan los paneles, calientan el agua para uso doméstico. De esta forma se ahorra combustible para calentar el agua.

Células solares de un laboratorio espacial

Paneles solares

Motores

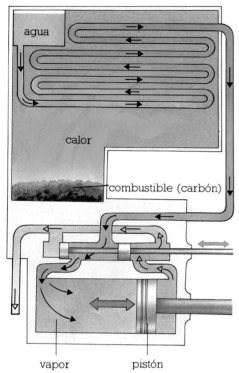

calor

agua

combustible (carbón)

vapor   pistón

Funcionamiento de una máquina de vapor

Locomotora de vapor

Motor de un avión de reacción

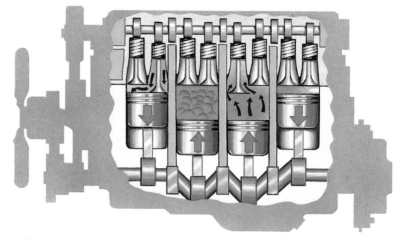

Sección transversal del motor de un coche. Se ven los cilindros, en los que se quema la gasolina

Los motores funcionan porque los gases producidos al arder un combustible originan unos movimientos de avance y de retroceso. En el motor de un coche se quema gasolina. Los gases producidos al quemar la gasolina impulsan los pistones del motor hacia arriba y luego hacia abajo. Al moverse los pistones, mueven las ruedas del coche. De esta forma, se mueve el coche.

En el motor de un camión se quema gasóleo. (El gasóleo y la gasolina salen del petróleo). Los gases producidos al quemarse el gasóleo mueven los pistones hacia arriba y hacia abajo. Al efectuar ese movimiento, los pistones mueven las ruedas del camión. En una máquina de vapor, el calor transforma el agua en vapor. Cuando el agua se transforma en vapor, se expande y ocupa un volumen mayor. La fuerza del vapor hace que los pistones suban y bajen. Los pistones mueven las ruedas, con las que se mueve la máquina.

En un motor de reacción se quema parafina de petróleo. La parafina inflamada, junto con el aire caliente y otros gases, salen por la parte trasera del motor, impulsando el avión hacia adelante.

Rozamiento

Mover cualquier cosa significa consumir energía. Es decir, que para hacer que las cosas se muevan se necesita disponer de energía. Si empujas un libro sobre una mesa, se deslizará sobre ella. El libro irá deteniéndose, hasta pararse completamente, debido al rozamiento. El rozamiento es un fenómeno de fricción que retarda y detiene el movimiento.

El niño de la figura está intentando mover la pesada caja por el suelo. Le resulta difícil porque hay mucho rozamiento de la caja con el suelo. Movería la caja con más facilidad si la colocara sobre unas ruedas o sobre unos rodillos. En ese caso habría menos rozamiento y el niño gastaría menos energía para mover la caja.

Muchas cosas se desplazan sobre ruedas. Las ruedas ayudan a mover cosas pesadas porque reducen la zona de rozamiento. El aceite y la grasa también reducen el rozamiento. Esas substancias resbaladizas permiten mover las cosas más fácilmente, puesto que disminuyen el rozamiento. El aceite y la grasa ahorran energía y evitan rechinamientos y desgastes.

Sin embargo, el rozamiento resulta muchas veces útil. Sin el rozamiento de nuestros pies en el suelo, no seríamos capaces de andar o correr. Las ruedas de un coche se agarran a la carretera a causa del rozamiento. Los frenos funcionan debido al rozamiento. Incluso las manos del conductor sujetan el volante debido al rozamiento.

Engrase de una bicicleta

Distintas clases de energía

Existen diferentes clases de energía. En el dibujo se ven algunas de ellas: energía calorífica, luminosa, eléctrica, química, motriz y acústica. También existe la energía nuclear o energía atómica.

Nosotros no podemos crear energía. Sólo podemos transformar una clase de energía en otra. Como hemos visto, la energía calorífica puede transformarse en energía eléctrica, por ejemplo en una central eléctrica que queme carbón. En nuestro cuerpo transformamos la energía química de los alimentos que comemos en energía calorífica y en energía motriz. Una llama transforma la energía química en energía calorífica y energía luminosa. Una radio transforma la energía eléctrica en energía acústica. Un aparato de televisión transforma la energía eléctrica en energía acústica y energía luminosa. La pila de una linterna transforma la energía química en energía eléctrica. Cuando montamos en una bicicleta provista de una dinamo, transformamos la energía motriz en electricidad. Esta electricidad hace que se encienda el faro de la bicicleta (energía luminosa).

La energía puede almacenarse

La energía puede almacenarse para ser utilizada posteriormente. Cuanta más energía se almacene mayor será el trabajo que se pueda realizar luego. El niño de la figura está dando cuerda a la hélice de su avión de juguete. Cuando da vueltas a la hélice, enrolla una tira de goma. Cuanto más enrolla el niño la goma, el avión volará más y a mayor velocidad. La tira de goma está acumulando la energía que luego hará volar al avión.

Cuando le damos cuerda a un reloj, lo que hacemos es almacenar energía en el resorte del reloj. Éste funcionará hasta que el resorte se haya desenrollado y toda la energía haya sido utilizada.

Combustibles como el carbón, el petróleo y el gas son también almacenes de energía. Lo es, igualmente, el alimento que comemos.

La batería de un coche acumula electricidad. Mientras el coche está en marcha, el motor mueve un generador, que produce electricidad.
La electricidad se almacena en la batería. Esa electricidad puede utilizarse luego para poner en marcha el coche o para encender sus luces o su radio. El carrito del repartidor de leche funciona con baterías (electricidad almacenada). Por la noche, el carrito se enchufa a la red del suministro eléctrico. Las baterías del carrito van almacenando, así, electricidad. Al día siguiente, la electricidad de las baterías hará funcionar el motor del carrito.

Batería de coche

Carrito del repartidor recargando las baterías

Ahorro de energía

Aislamiento de la pared de una casa

Estos coches están diseñados para consumir menos gasolina

Es importante que no agotemos nuestras reservas de energía. No podemos dejar de utilizar petróleo, gasolina, gas, carbón o electricidad, pero debemos utilizarlos cuidadosamente. Podemos evitar las pérdidas que se producen en la calefacción de casa y del colegio. Las puertas y ventanas abiertas o mal cerradas dejan escapar un calor valioso. Podríamos llevar ropa de más abrigo, incluso dentro de las casas. Podríamos apagar las luces y desconectar los aparatos eléctricos al terminar de usarlos.

Puede ahorrarse mucho calor y, por tanto, combustible mediante un buen aislamiento. Se pierde mucho calor a través de los techos, las paredes y las ventanas de los edificios. Estas pérdidas de calor pueden reducirse, o evitarse, aislando las paredes y los techos. Las ventanas con dobles cristales no dejan pasar tanto calor como las de cristal sencillo.

El consumo de gasolina puede reducirse comprando coches más pequeños. Los coches pequeños y ligeros gastan menos combustible que los grandes y pesados. Los coches aerodinámicos consumen menos gasolina que los que no lo son.

Una forma aún mejor de ahorrar combustible es andar o montar en bicicleta. Además de no contaminar la atmósfera, es más sano.

¿Te acuerdas?

(Si no sabes las respuestas, búscalas en las páginas anteriores.)

1 Nombra seis usos distintos de la electricidad en las casas.

2 ¿Por qué es mejor, a veces, utilizar electricidad que carbón, petróleo u otros combustibles?

3 ¿Dónde se produce la electricidad que empleamos en nuestras casas?

4 ¿Cómo se llama la gran rueda movida por el vapor en las centrales eléctricas?

5 ¿Cómo se llama la máquina que, al girar, produce electricidad?

6 ¿Cómo se llama la central eléctrica que utiliza el agua de los ríos de corriente rápida para producir electricidad?

7 ¿Qué combustible utiliza una central nuclear?

8 Cita otras dos formas de producir electricidad.

9 ¿Para qué sirven los paneles solares?

10 ¿Cómo utilizan las naves espaciales la energía solar?

11 ¿Para qué puede utilizarse el agua caliente subterránea que hay cerca de los volcanes?

12 ¿Cómo funciona el motor de un coche?

13 ¿Cómo funciona un motor de reacción?

14 ¿Qué es el rozamiento?

15 ¿Qué podemos hacer para que haya menos rozamiento?

16 Nombra tres casos en los que el rozamiento nos es útil.

17 Nombra cinco clases de energía.

18 ¿En qué convierte una llama la energía química?

19 ¿Dónde almacenamos energía cuando le damos cuerda a un reloj?

20 Cita algunas formas de ahorrar energía en nuestras casas.

Cosas para hacer

1 **La electricidad en casa.** Reúne fotos y dibujos de todos los aparatos domésticos que funcionan gracias a la electricidad. Haz un cartel con las fotos y dibujos. Intenta averiguar cuánta electricidad consume cada uno. El consumo de la electricidad se mide en vatios o en kilovatios (un kilovatio es igual a 1.000 vatios). En una bombilla, por ejemplo, verás escrito 60 vatios, 100 vatios, etc., y en una aspiradora 375 vatios, 500 vatios, etc.

Junto a cada foto de tu cartel anota su consumo de electricidad. ¿Qué aparatos de tu casa consumen más electricidad? ¿Cuáles consumen menos?

2   Lee el contador eléctrico. El contador eléctrico de tu casa indica la electricidad que se ha consumido. Dile a una persona mayor que te ayude a leer el contador de tu casa. Hay dos tipos principales de contador. Los dibujos te muestran la lectura de ayer y la de hoy. Si restas el número menor, que corresponde a la lectura de ayer, del número mayor, que es la lectura de hoy, sabrás cuánta electricidad se ha consumido desde ayer.

Lee el contador de tu casa hoy. Anota la cantidad. Vuelve a leerlo mañana a la misma hora. Calcula cuánta electricidad se ha gastado. Lee el contador en un día caluroso y vuelve a leerlo en un día frío. ¿Cuánta electricidad se gasta en tu casa, en 24 horas, con tiempo caluroso y con tiempo frío?

¿Cuánto cuesta la electricidad en tu ciudad? Mira alguna factura de electricidad para averiguarlo.

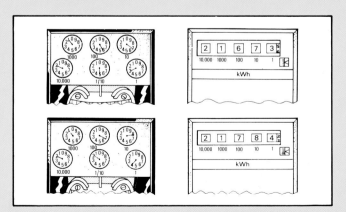

3   Ferrocarriles. Muchas compañías de ferrocarriles han cambiado los trenes de vapor por trenes movidos por gasóelo o por electricidad. ¿Por qué habrán cambiado?

4   Uso de ciertas energías. ¿Por qué no es posible siempre utilizar la energía del sol, del viento o de las mareas?

5   Desgaste. ¿Sabes por qué las puntas de los lápices se hacen cada vez más cortas, las alfombras y los felpudos se vuelven más finos, las suelas de los zapatos se agujerean, los neumáticos pierden su dibujo y el papel de lija y las escobas se desgastan? ¿Cómo llamamos al fenómeno que hace que las cosas se desgasten de esa forma?

6   El rozamiento produce calor. Consigue un clavo largo. Toca su punta. ¿Qué sensación da? Ahora frota el clavo rápidamente, hacia adelante y hacia atrás, sobre un ladrillo o sobre un trozo de cemento. Vuelve a tocar la punta. ¿Notas alguna diferencia?

7   El rozamiento produce calor. En tiempo frío, frótate las manos ligeramente. ¿Las notas más calientes? Ponte las manos en la cara. ¿Notas más calientes las manos? Ahora, frótate las palmas de las manos con más fuerza. ¿Se calientan más? Ponlas en tu cara para comprobarlo. Eso se debe a que el rozamiento produce calor. Cuanto más rozamiento, más calor.

8 Los frenos. Los frenos funcionan gracias al rozamiento. Intenta averiguar cómo actúan los frenos de una bicicleta. ¿De qué son las zapatas del freno de una bicicleta? ¿Por qué no funcionan los frenos si están manchados de aceite o de grasa?

9 Carreteras con hielo y otras cosas. Explica qué relación hay entre las siguientes cosas y el rozamiento:

- Echamos arena en las carreteras cuando hay placas de hielo.

- Podemos patinar sobre el hielo.

- Ponemos una alfombrilla de goma en la bañera.

- Cuando encendemos una cerilla, la frotamos sobre una cara lateral de la caja.

Si echas un poco de polvos de talco sobre las cartas de una baraja, no se adhieren tanto unas a otras.

Ponemos aceite a las partes móviles de los coches, bicicletas y otras máquinas.

10 Petróleo. Las palabras «prospección», «lubrificar» y «crudo» se emplean frecuentemente cuando la gente habla del petróleo. Busca en el diccionario el significado de estas palabras. Escribe una frase que incluya estas palabras.

11 Construye un helicóptero de juguete. Los helicópteros de verdad vuelan por efecto del chorro de aire que unas potentes hélices lanzan hacia abajo.

Para construir un helicóptero de juguete necesitas un globo, un trozo de cartón y un tapón de corcho. Escoge un tapón de corcho que encaje bien en la boca del globo. Recorta en el cartón un disco de unos 10 cm de diámetro y haz en el centro un agujero de unos 3 mm de diámetro. Haz otro agujero del mismo diámetro en el tapón de corcho y pega éste al disco de cartón, de forma que los dos agujeros estén enfrente el uno del otro.

Dile a un amigo que sujete el disco mientras tú hinchas el globo. Mantén cerrado el cuello del globo con dos dedos de una mano, mientras

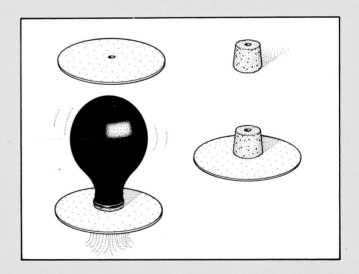

abres la boca del globo e introduces el corcho, con la ayuda de tu amigo.

Coloca tu modelo sobre una superficie lisa y suelta el cuello del globo. Dale un ligero empujoncito a la parte inferior del helicóptero y observa si se mantiene flotando mientras el aire sale del globo.

Observa lo alto que sube tu helicóptero cuando está poco lleno y cuando está muy lleno.

¿Se desplaza tu helicóptero sobre una superficie rugosa? ¿Flota por encima del agua?

¿De dónde proviene la energía que necesita tu helicóptero para desplazarse?

12   Barriles. ¿Has observado que muchos líquidos, como la cerveza y el petróleo, se envasan en barriles? Piensa por qué lo harán así. ¿Por qué no se envasan en recipientes rectangulares?

13   Rodamientos de bolas. Se utilizan rodamientos de bolas para conseguir que algunas cosas se desplacen suavemente. ¿Puedes explicar lo que hacen las bolas? El experimento 5 de la página 28 puede ayudarte a entenderlo. ¿Conoces algunos objetos en los que se empleen rodamientos de bolas?

14   Secadores de pelo. Dile a una persona mayor que te enseñe y ponga en marcha un secador de pelo. Nota el aire que sale de él. ¿Qué sensación produce? Escucha el ruido que produce el secador.

Coloca unos trocitos de papel frente al secador. ¿Qué sucede con ellos?

¿Qué clase de energía es la que emplea el secador de pelo? ¿Qué nuevas clases de energía produce el secador de pelo?

Experimentos

Realiza los experimentos cuidadosamente. Escribe lo que has hecho y lo que ocurre. Cuenta en casa o en clase lo que has aprendido. Compara tus descubrimientos con los de tus amigos.

1   Haz un tanque con un carrete de hilo

Lo que necesitas: Un carrete de hilo; una banda de goma; un clipe; un palito de bombón helado; una rodaja de vela sin el pábilo y una regla.

Lo que puedes hacer: Pasa la banda de goma por el orificio del carrete de hilo y fija un extremo con el clipe.

Haz un orificio en el centro de la rodaja de vela y pasa por él la banda de goma. A continuación, pasa el palito de bombón helado por la vuelta del extremo de la banda de goma.

Enrolla la banda de goma, dándole vueltas al palito de bombón helado. Coloca el tanque en el suelo y observa si se pone en movimiento.

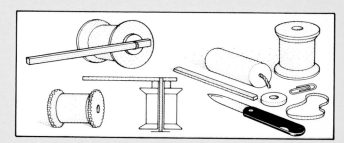

Mira qué distancia recorre. Dale una vuelta al palito y mide con la regla la distancia que recorre. A continuación repite la operación, pero esta vez dale dos vueltas al palito; y así sucesivamente.

Refleja tus resultados en un gráfico como éste:

Gráfico de resultados

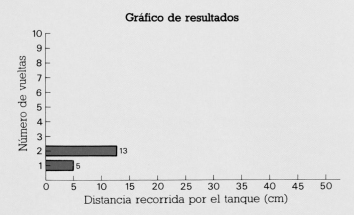

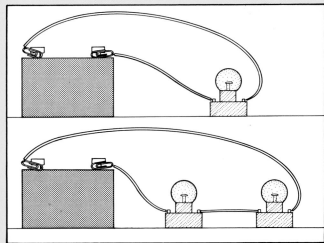

Mira la distancia que recorre tu tanque en diferentes superficies, tales como una alfombra, un trozo de madera sin pulir y un suelo liso.

¿Funciona mejor el tanque si haces unas pequeñas muescas, *con cuidado,* en los bordes del carrete de hilo, con una navaja? ¿Por qué marcha ahora mejor?

¿Qué pendiente puede subir tu tanque?

2   ¿Qué sucede cuando se conectan bombillas de linterna a una pila?

Lo que necesitas: Una pila de 4,5 voltios; cuatro bombillas de linterna en sus correspondientes portalámparas; seis trozos de cable eléctrico recubierto de plástico, de unos 15 cm de longitud cada uno; unas tijeras; un destornillador pequeño y dos clipes.

Lo que puedes hacer: Con`la ayuda de las tijeras deja al descubierto los extremos de los trozos de cable. Quita uno o dos centímetros del recubrimiento de plástico.

Toma dos trozos de cable y sujeta en uno de los extremos de cada uno un clipe. Fija cada clipe en uno de los bornes de la pila.

Con el destornillador conecta los extremos libres de los dos trozos de cable a los dos bornes del portalámparas. Ya dispones de un circuito eléctrico. Cuando se encienda la bombilla, observa si brilla mucho o poco. Si no se enciende la bombilla, comprueba las conexiones.

A continuación conecta la pila a dos bombillas en sus correspondientes portalámparas, como se muestra en la figura. Comprueba si las bombillas brillan ahora más o menos que en el experimento anterior. Comprueba luego si la pila puede hacer que se enciendan tres o cuatro bombillas al mismo tiempo.

¿Qué influencia tiene el número de bombillas sobre el mayor o menor brillo de la luz?

¿Qué pasa si desenroscas un poco una de las bombillas? ¿Sabes por qué una bombilla defectuosa en un árbol de Navidad hace que no se encienda ninguna?

¿Qué pasa si conectas ahora dos bombillas a la pila, pero teniendo otra vez cada bombilla su propio circuito? Las figuras te indican cómo realizar el circuito.

3 ¿Qué sucede cuando dos pilas alimentan una bombilla de linterna?

Lo que necesitas: Una bombilla de linterna con su portalámparas; dos trozos de cable eléctrico recubierto de plástico; unas tijeras; un destornillador pequeño; tres pilas de 1,5 voltios cada una; cinta adhesiva y dos clipes.

Lo que puedes hacer: Con la ayuda de las tijeras quita unos 2 cm del recubrimiento de plástico de cada uno de los extremos de los trozos de cable.

Con el destornillador conecta uno de los extremos de cada cable a cada borne del portalámparas. Fija un clipe a cada uno de los otros extremos de los cables.

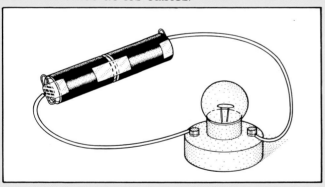

Sujeta con cinta adhesiva los clipes a una pila de linterna: uno de los clipes, al saliente de la parte superior de la pila; el otro, a la base metálica de la misma.

¿Se enciende la bombilla? ¿Brilla mucho o poco?

Luego, une con cinta adhesiva dos pilas, de forma que el saliente de una de ellas quede unido a la base metálica de la otra. Fija los clipes de los extremos de los cables a las dos pilas unidas. La figura te muestra la forma de hacerlo. ¿Brilla ahora la bombilla más o menos que antes?

Hazlo, a continuación, con tres pilas unidas entre sí. ¿Qué sucede? ¿Brilla más o menos la bombilla?

4 Energía magnética

La energía magnética es una de las muchas clases de energía. En este experimento vamos a ver el máximo grosor de material que atraviesa la energía magnética.

Lo que necesitas: Un imán; varios clipes de acero; unas tarjetas postales; otros materiales, por ejemplo, madera, cartón, cartulina, plástico, goma y vidrio, y una regla.

Lo que puedes hacer: Echa algunos clipes sobre una cartulina. Mueve el imán por debajo de ella. ¿Qué sucede con los clipes? ¿Atraviesa el magnetismo la cartulina?

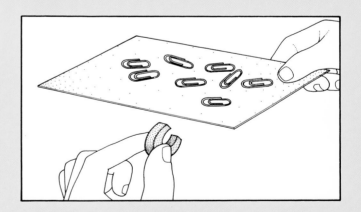

Repite ahora el experimento con dos cartulinas, colocadas una encima de la otra. ¿Atraviesa el magnetismo las dos cartulinas? Repite el experimento añadiendo cada vez una cartulina más. ¿Qué sucede? ¿Cuál es el mayor grosor que puede atravesar el magnetismo?

Prueba con otros materiales. Comprueba cuáles de ellos atraviesa el magnetismo y cuáles no. ¿Pasa el magnetismo a través de espesores mayores de algunos materiales que de otros?

¿Pasa el magnetismo a través del agua? ¿Pasa a través de tu mano? Necesitarás un imán potente para comprobarlo.

5   Cómo facilitan el trabajo las ruedas

Lo que necesitas: Tres o cuatro ladrillos; varias canicas del mismo tamaño; una tapa de hojalata; un trozo de cuerda delgada y un dinamómetro de uso doméstico.

Lo que puedes hacer: Ata la cuerda a un ladrillo. Tira de él, arrastrándolo sobre una superficie lisa, y comprueba la fuerza que tienes que hacer.

Amarra luego el extremo de la cuerda al dinamómetro y observa qué fuerza indica éste en el momento en que el ladrillo comienza a moverse.

Pon unas canicas dentro de una tapa de hojalata, y sobre ésta, el ladrillo. Con el dinamómetro fíjate qué fuerza marca éste en el momento en que el ladrillo comienza a moverse. ¿Tienes que hacer ahora más o menos fuerza que antes?

Repite el experimento con dos ladrillos, uno encima de otro. Haz la prueba primero sólo con los ladrillos, y luego con éstos apoyados en la tapa llena de canicas. Repite el experimento con tres ladrillos y luego con cuatro.

Con los resultados que obtengas, haz un gráfico como éste:

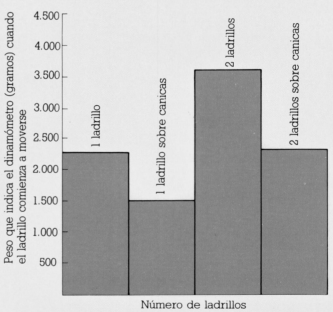

6   ¿Cómo absorben los diferentes colores los rayos de sol?

Lo que necesitas: Dos termómetros iguales; unas hojas de papel, del mismo tamaño pero de diferentes colores.

Lo que puedes hacer: Deja los dos termómetros a la luz del sol, cerca uno del otro. Cuida que ambos termómetros estén sobre el mismo tipo de superficie. ¿Qué temperatura marcan?

Tapa un termómetro con una hoja de papel negro y el otro con una hoja de papel blanco. Déjalos así, a la luz del sol, de 15 a 20 minutos.

Quita rápidamente las dos hojas de papel y observa qué temperatura marca cada termómetro. ¿Bajo qué hoja de papel marca la temperatura más elevada? ¿Bajo qué hoja de papel marca la temperatura más baja? ¿Qué color absorbe, o retiene, más los rayos de sol?

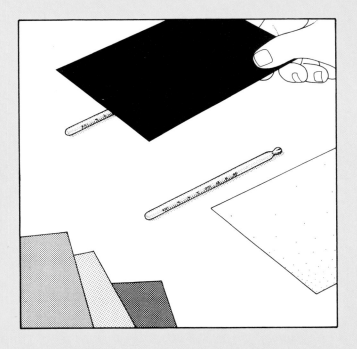

Repite ahora el experimento con hojas de papel de otros colores. Ensáyalo también con una hoja de papel blanco áspero y con otra hoja de papel blanco brillante.

¿Qué color de ropa sería el más apropiado en tiempo frío? ¿Y cuál el más apropiado en tiempo de calor?

Si no puedes hacer este experimento a la luz del sol, puedes realizarlo a la luz y al calor desprendidos por una lámpara portátil. Asegúrate de que la luz dé por igual en las dos hojas de papel.

7   Substancias aislantes del calor

Las substancias que conservan el calor, retrasando el enfriamiento, se llaman aislantes del calor.

Lo que necesitas: Dos botes de hojalata del mismo tamaño, provistos de sus correspondientes tapas; dos termómetros; papel de periódico;

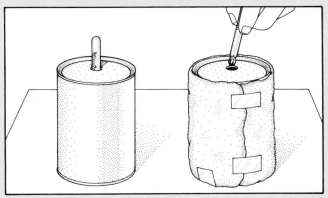

algodón; filtro; tela de lana; piel; nailon; cinta adhesiva y un reloj.

Lo que puedes hacer: Haz en la tapa de cada bote un agujero que permita introducir por él un termómetro.

Coloca los botes sobre una mesa, uno junto al otro. Pon un paño de mesa o varias capas de papel de periódico debajo de los botes para preservar la mesa.

Con cinta adhesiva pon una capa de algodón en rama alrededor de un bote. El otro déjalo como está.

Destapa los dos botes. Dile a tu profesor que los llene de agua algo caliente. El agua de los dos botes debe estar a la misma temperatura. Llena ambos botes exactamente hasta la misma altura. Pon *con cuidado* las tapas de los botes e introduce un termómetro en cada agujero.

Toma la temperatura del agua de cada bote cada diez minutos. Dibuja un gráfico que muestre cómo se enfría el agua de cada bote. Emplea colores diferentes para el gráfico correspondiente a cada bote. ¿Qué bote se enfría antes?

Repite el experimento, colocando ahora algodón en rama alrededor de un bote y tela de lana, o papel de periódico, alrededor del otro. ¿Qué bote se enfría antes? ¿Cuál tarda más en enfriarse?

Realiza el experimento con otros materiales. De todos ellos, ¿cuál es el que consigue que el calor dure más tiempo? Este material es el mejor aislante.

8 ¿Cuál es la forma mejor para un barco?

Si queremos que un barco o un avión gasten el menor combustible posible, hay que tener muy en cuenta la forma que les damos. En este experimento vamos a averiguar cuál es la forma más adecuada para un barco.

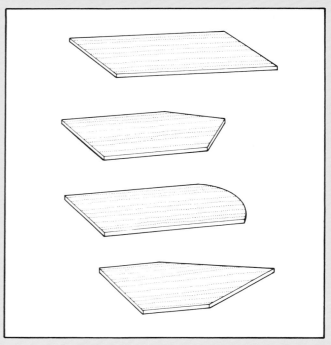

Lo que necesitas: Dos planchas rectangulares de madera, ambas del mismo tamaño. Un tamaño bueno puede ser de 12 a 14 cm de largo y de unos 6 cm de ancho. Necesitas, además, dos cáncamos pequeños; dos clipes; hilo de nailon; una cubeta de plástico; una sierra; papel de lija; un juego de pesas; plastilina y unas arandelas pequeñas.

Lo que puedes hacer: Corta, *con cuidado,* con la sierra, una de las planchas de madera, para darle una de las formas que ves en la figura. Deja la otra plancha con su forma rectangular original.

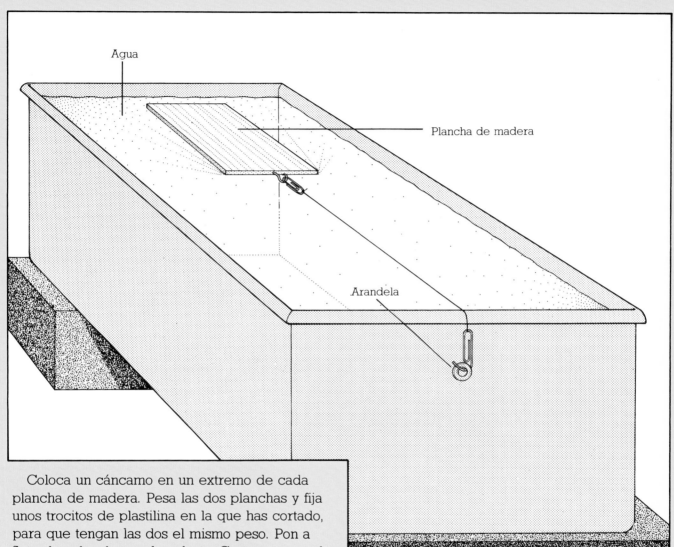

Agua

Plancha de madera

Arandela

Coloca un cáncamo en un extremo de cada plancha de madera. Pesa las dos planchas y fija unos trocitos de plastilina en la que has cortado, para que tengan las dos el mismo peso. Pon a flotar las planchas en la cubeta. Corta un trozo de hilo de nailon, de una longitud algo mayor que la de la cubeta. Ata un clipe a cada extremo de hilo.

Deposita sobre el agua, en un extremo de la cubeta, la plancha de madera rectangular, es decir, la que no has cortado. Engancha uno de los clipes en el cáncamo. En el otro clipe cuelga una arandela y tensa el hilo de nailon. El barco comenzará a deslizarse sobre el agua. Si no lo hiciera, cuelga más arandelas, hasta que se mueva.

Cronometra el tiempo que tarda el barco en recorrer toda la cubeta, desde un extremo al otro. Cronometra luego el otro barco, empleando la misma longitud de hilo, los mismos clipes y las mismas arandelas.

¿Qué barco se desplaza más rápido?

Si estos barcos fuesen de verdad, ¿cuál de ellos necesitaría menos energía para navegar?

Glosario

Aquí tienes el significado de algunas palabras que quizá hayas encontrado por primera vez en este libro:

Aislante: Material que se emplea para conservar una determinada temperatura. Los aislantes producen una sensación agradablemente templada al tacto.

Batería: Acumulador de electricidad.

Célula solar: Aparato que recoge la luz del sol y la convierte en energía eléctrica.

Central eléctrica: Edificio o fábrica de grandes dimensiones donde se produce electricidad.

Central hidroeléctrica: Central eléctrica que utiliza la fuerza del agua en movimiento para girar sus generadores y producir electricidad.

Central nuclear (llamada también central atómica): Central eléctrica que utiliza la energía de un mineral llamado uranio, que se encuentra en algunas rocas, para producir electricidad.

Combustible: Todo lo que puede arder.

Dióxido de carbono: Uno de los gases componentes del aire. El aire que nosotros, y otros seres vivos, expulsamos al respirar contiene dióxido de carbono. Los vegetales utilizan el dióxido de carbono para fabricar su alimento.

Doble acristalamiento: Se dice de la ventana que tiene dos cristales, entre los que queda una capa de aire.

Energía: El «motor» de las cosas. La energía es necesaria para realizar cualquier trabajo o movimiento.

Evaporarse: Cuando el agua se calienta, desaparece en el aire en forma de vapor de agua. Decimos, entonces, que el agua se ha evaporado.

Generador: Máquina que produce electricidad. También se le llama dinamo.

Oxígeno: Gas que se encuentra en el aire y que va a la sangre cuando aspiramos, al respirar. El oxígeno transforma los alimentos que tomamos, con lo que se produce energía. El oxígeno es necesario para que un objeto arda.

Paneles solares: Placas que recogen la energía solar y la emplean para calentar agua.

Pistones: Cilindros metálicos cortos que están situados dentro de unos tubos y que se mueven hacia arriba y hacia abajo en el interior del mismo.

Rozamiento: Acción de frotamiento, que va frenando el movimiento, hasta llegar a detener el objeto.

Turbina: Rueda de grandes dimensiones que gira por efecto del agua en movimiento o del vapor; la turbina mueve los generadores de una central eléctrica y éstos producen electricidad.

Vapor de agua: Gas invisible que se forma al calentar agua.